George and Maggie
and the
Red Light Saloon

George and Maggie and the

Red Light Saloon

❖

Depravation, Debauchery, Violence, And Sundry Cussedness In A Kansas Cowtown

Nonfiction by Rod Cook

iUniverse, Inc.
New York Lincoln Shanghai

GEORGE AND MAGGIE AND THE RED LIGHT SALOON
Depravation, Debauchery, Violence, And Sundry Cussedness In A Kansas Cowtown

iUniverse, Inc.

For information address:
iUniverse, Inc.
2021 Pine Lake Road, Suite 100
Lincoln, NE 68512
www.iuniverse.com

ISBN: 0-595-29407-3

Printed in the United States of America

For

Norma White

and

The People of
The Border Queen

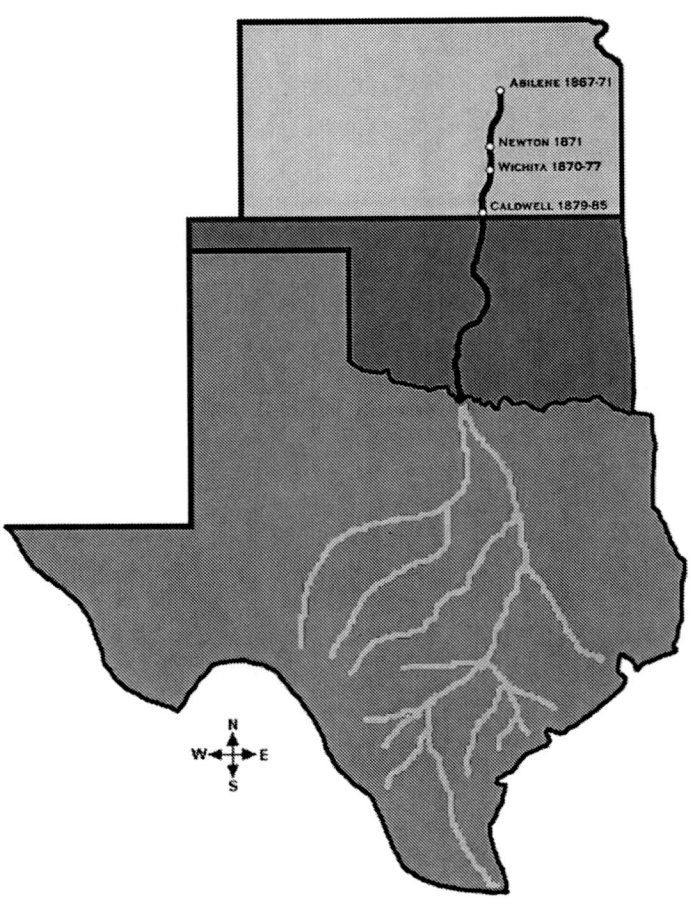

Chisholm Trail and Texas feeder trails

Contents

ACKNOWLEDGMENTS

Among those whose help and encouragement was instrumental in the completion of this work were authors Troy Boucher and Bill O'Neal whose editorial reviews, insights, and advice have proven invaluable; and Computer graphics wizard Rod Michael of Cheney, Kansas who fabricated the cover graphic from a number of ideas composed in my head. The materials he used were provided by several special people: Gloria White of Caldwell, Kansas, loaned several photographs from her extensive archives—among them, the street scene of old Caldwell utilized in the cover art. "Maggie's garter" was meticulously created by Lois Croft of Clearwater, Kansas. Special thanks to Len Gratteri of Hillsboro, Oregon, by whose kind gesture the actual famous sixgun belonging to Caldwell Deputy Marshal Ben Wheeler appears in the cover graphic.

I am indebted to Marilyn Houlden of Caldwell who proofread the manuscript. Also to historian/writer/researcher Edward Herring of Mt. Hope, Arkansas who graciously shared research and sources on Maggie's early background before 1875. He, along with historian Fred Strickland of South Haven, Kansas, provided particulars drawn from their extensive knowledge of the history of Hunnewell, Kansas.

I also wish to thank researcher Hershul King of Fort Worth, Texas, for his help in my search for Maggie in the Dallas/Fort Worth area and historian June Westphal of Eureka Springs, Arkansas, for her search there.

I would also like to acknowledge my new email friend, John Gillon of Lewisville, North Carolina, who, at the time of this writing, is still searching for Maggie among his ancestors.

A NOTE TO THE READER

Located just two miles from the Oklahoma Indian Territory, Caldwell, Kansas, known as "The Border Queen" in her early rowdy days, was the last Kansas cowtown on the Chisholm Trail. While not as well known as Abilene, Ellsworth, Dodge City and some of the other cowtowns that gained notoriety through books and movies, Caldwell too, had her tough characters and tumultuous times. Indeed, the Border Queen was a rough place to be—wild, riotous, unruly, and violent. But somehow her noteworthy characters were circumvented in the early dime novels and subsequent movies that popularized those places and made the names Earp, Hickok, Masterson and Holliday recognizable to successive generations.

The aim of this book is to introduce to those interested in true western history a slice of the little known past of Caldwell, now a quiet little city whose true stature in the ranks of the cowtowns has not yet been recognized.

This book started out to be a short research project—I wanted to know a little more about a couple of Caldwell's early notorious characters—just a little digging that I do every now and then only to satisfy my own curiosity. But as more information was uncovered, it grew beyond my expectations. By the time I had exhausted all of my leads to any further insight, it had become what you now hold before you. Hopefully, it will be of interest to you and perhaps to a future historian or two. I have composed the information in chronological order and as much as possible, have let the extracts and articles set the pace and tell the story. In several places where voids exist in the extant record I have offered some speculative suggestions as possible explanations. Where I stray from pure nonfiction in those few places, I have done so in a manner that I hope the reader can readily distinguish from the factual information.

Mrs. Norma White, President of the Caldwell Historical Society at the time of this writing, shared my curiosity and it is because of her great interest that I was motivated to seriously pursue the information that composes this book. It is to her that I respectfully offer this work.

It was not my intent to sensationalize this story although the material here could very well be shaped into an exceptional historical novel. I invite others with skills greater than my own to investigate that possibility. Many amazing true stories are to be found in the rich history of the Border Queen—any one of which is worthy of a romanticized novel or movie script. One of these is the story of *George and Maggie and The Red Light Saloon*.

Rod Cook
May, 2003

INTRODUCTION

During the Civil War, Texas cattle could not be sold at the established markets in the northern states. As a result, the herds proliferated to such an extent that by the end of the war, Texas beef could be had for less than a dollar a head. Herds were left to run wild on the vast Texas range, unbranded, untended and unclaimed. After the war, men could simply lay claim to as many head as they were capable of rounding up. The state had over 3,000,000 head of cattle—but no market.

A farsighted young man named Joseph McCoy recognized the great opportunity and grasped it. After scouting the newly laid Union Pacific rail line west of Kansas City he chose a tiny hamlet called Abilene to be his terminus. There, in 1867, at McCoy's urging, the railroad built a siding. McCoy purchased 250 acres of land, built a hotel and cattle pens and then spread the word. Soon, strong willed Texas men, utilizing an obscure trail blazed by a man named Jesse Chisholm, also seized the opportunity and began driving their herds, nearly worthless in Texas, to Abilene, the portal of a fantastic eastern market.

Like tributaries of a great river, many lesser trails originating from all over the heart of Texas and from as far south as Brownsville converged to ascend the great trail. Several million head of longhorn cattle traversed its length between 1867 and

1885 as well as countless freight wagons traveling both ways. Leaving civilization behind at a place called Red River Station, the drovers threaded their way northward through the unsettled and hostile country they called "The Nations"—Oklahoma Indian Territory.

Wending through this perilous country they endured unimaginable hardships and braved untold perils. At the mercy of the land, the weather and the Indians, and often times renegade whites as well, few vestiges of white habitation were encountered. The several remote outposts that they did pass through along the way had names straight out of a colorful western novel: Bull Foot, Buffalo Springs, Skeleton Ranch, and Polecat Creek among others.

Haggard and weary after several months of bad food, dust, stampedes and having conquered innumerable abusive deprivations, they emerged from the hostile Indian Territory at the upstart little town of Caldwell—a welcome reprieve at the first real civilization to be encountered since leaving Texas.

As the trail continued northward into the infant state of Kansas, it gave birth to other new towns that fed upon its vitality. Finally, the herds flooded Abilene and McCoy's dreams were realized.

McCoy's was the first of countless commercial enterprises that capitalized on the cattle drives that came up to Kansas over the Chisholm Trail. The route became the first great artery that brought the torrents of longhorns—the life's blood that built and nourished fledgling central Kansas.

The railroad drew the cattle and the cowboys to Abilene. And with the cattle and the cowboys came eager entrepreneurs who shared McCoy's dream and Abilene became the first of the great Kansas cowtowns on the Chisholm Trail.

It was the end of a daunting journey for the cowboys as they delivered the herds to new owners. The cowboys were paid there—most with more money than they had ever accumulated altogether at one time. They were primed for celebration and the money and whiskey flowed, good times prevailed and the town boomed with all of the good and the bad that the cattle and cowboys brought—until the cattle season of 1872 when the railroad met the herds in Newton. It was a story that would be played over and over again.

Then, Newton became the first railhead and closest shipping point and Newton became the exalted portal and boomed as Abilene had. Newton was to become a little larger, a little busier, and a little more rowdy than Abilene. But Newton's heyday was short-lived. Soon it could be seen that a pattern was beginning to develop and that Newton, as a cowtown, was to be but a stepping stone as the rails progressed southward.

Wichita was next.

This narrative begins in Wichita in its formative cowtown era, bigger, busier, and rowdier yet. It will attempt to illuminate and put into perspective the little that has been written of the history and events surrounding George and Maggie Wood, a young couple who were, as were so many others, caught up in the excitement of the times, striving to carve out a portion of the windfall brought by the cattlemen. By virtue of the professions they chose, they were destined to become principals of a saga that rivals any told in the annals of the old west. Their vocation led them to Caldwell, Kansas, the establishment of the Red Light Saloon, tumultuous times, and extreme notoriety.

◆   ◆   ◆

"There were over 40 professional
gamblers in Caldwell…

   …and two small churches."

From the reminisces of
Grant Harris who, in
1880 at age 15, went
to work as a printer at
the Caldwell *Post*.

1

When the rails reached Wichita, Whitney Rupp, a Kansas City gambler, was one of many coming to seek a livelihood from the resulting Wichita boom. He is said to have commented, "the wages of sin are a damned sight better than the wages of virtue" and opened his magnificent two story Keno House on the northwest corner of Douglas and Main in Wichita. It was reputed to be the most elegant gambling and drinking establishment west of the Mississippi. Next door to the Keno House was Ab Pryor's Saloon where James Earp, older brother of Wyatt Earp worked as a bartender. Two blocks west was Wichita's bawdy district of the 1870's. It was in this environment that George and Maggie served their apprenticeship. In the first half of that decade, when George was barely 20 and Maggie was still in her teens, they learned survival in that venal quarter of society and became skilled in all the licentious stratagems of the sleaze peddler's trades.

The seedy district started at the intersection of Douglas Avenue and Water Street, known as "Horse Thief Corner", and ran north on Water. The house at Number 33 was known as "Bessie Earp's whorehouse."[1] Bessie was Wyatt Earp's sister-in-law, the wife of James Earp. On June 3, 1874, Constable J.W. McCartney served a warrant for the arrest of Bessie and Sallie Earp. They had been named in a complaint as having:

1

...unlawfully and feloniously set up and [kept] a bawdy house or brothel and did appear and act as mistress and have the care and management of a certain one story frame building situated and located North of Douglas Avenue near the bridge leading across the Arkansas River used and kept by said parties as a house of prostitution. From the wording of the charge it is seen that their "house" was the one story building at the rear of Doc Black's Riverside Hotel, north of Douglas and near the river.[2]

Much has been written outlining the Earps' activities in Wichita. There is general agreement that the Earp women were in the business of conducting business with male clients but many areas remain cloudy and thus engender various differing accounts. However, the 1875 census and Wichita court records ascertain that James, Bessie, Wyatt and Sallie Earp were living in Wichita at that time as well as 6 other girls using the Earp name. Also found in that census is the first mention of George and Maggie Wood, the young couple, that in the not too distant future, would bring havoc to the infant town of Caldwell.

Ed Bartholomew, in *Wyatt Earp—The Untold Story*, contends that Bessie Earp was listed as "head of household" in that 1875 census.[3] He also says, "George and Mag Woods of Caldwell Redlight fame started in the business under sponsorship of Bessie Earp."[4]

A close reading of the 1875 census appears to be partially contrary to Bartholomew's view. A short study of that census can lead to a different conclusion concerning the "head of household" status. The census sheet is in the form of vertically lined columns requiring the entry of 29 specific subjects of information concerning each individual, family, or household. A column was not provided in which to specifically denote the *Head of Household*. Instead, the established procedure dictated that the head of household was the *first person* listed. The fidelity of information that the census takers entered is found to be sadly lacking in the 1875, as well as '80, and '85 censuses. Typically, the 1875 census enumerator provided information in only seven of the 29 columns leaving the others blank.

The 1875 federal census lists the occupants of that notorious house on page 23 in the section entitled *Inhabitants in the City of Wichita*:

> Geo Wood, Age 18, Female, White, Profession: Sporting, Real estate valued at $300, Place of Birth: Arkansas, To Kansas from: Arkansas

> Laura Smith, Age 25, Female, White, Profession: Sporting, Place of birth: Indiana, To Kansas from: Missouri

> Geo. B Wood, Age 21, Male, White, Profession: Laborer, Place of birth: Texas, To Kansas from: Canada

> Bessie Earp, Age 32, Female, White, Profession: Sporting, Place of birth: New York, To Kansas from: Iowa

In reading that census, it is evident that confusion existed during the question/answer dialog between the enumerator and female "Geo." Why "Geo" was recorded twice, first as a female, 18, sporting, then "Geo B" afterward as male, 21, Laborer, is unknown. The female "Geo" was not *specifically* listed as head of household but *was* listed in the *first* position. Maggie Wood is listed in the 1880 census as age 23 and in the 1885 census as 28, so the female "Geo" fits age-wise to be Maggie Wood. In question is the information recorded in the *place of birth* column that lists her as being born in Arkansas. The 1880 and '85 censuses show her to have been born in Georgia as does the 1860 Georgia census. Why such errors appear in the information concerning George and Maggie is a perplexing and insoluble question. In the final analysis, though, considering all available information, it must be concluded that the female "Geo" was Maggie Wood. The fact that Maggie was listed first, denoting her as "head of household", could very well indicate that she was the proprietress of the house at that time.

The age shown for male "Geo B" in the '75 census varies a year from that shown in the '80 census and the date inscribed on his tombstone. Even so, "Geo B" is undoubtedly the real George. His middle initial, "B", and place of birth check out on the '80 census and on his tombstone which shows his date of birth as 21 March 1853, his place of birth as Owen Sound, Canada, and age at death as 28. Confusion over his last name has resulted in many references to him as *Woods*. His actual surname is "Wood."

Maggie was born *Margaret Ann Gillon* in Georgia in 1856 or '57. By 1865 her father, Isaac, had moved his family to Lafayette Township, Sebastian County, Arkansas. In the 1870 census, the nine member Gillon family is found living in Towanda Township, Butler County, Kansas, about twenty miles north-east of Wichita.[5] Because she was many times referred to as "Mag" in newspaper accounts and, particularly, in early pioneer George Freeman's 1892 book about early day Caldwell, *Midnight and Noonday*, Maggie is today generally referred to by most as "Mag." But as evidenced by numerous records, she preferred *Maggie*.

Sometime between her 13th and 18th birthdays Maggie left home. Once in Wichita, she may not have "fallen" right away. She may have tried working at legitimate employment up to and even after meeting George Wood. If she worked as a prostitute before 1875 she most likely used an assumed name, as was the common practice of young prostitutes desiring to insure anonymity or seclusion from their families. It is unlikely that she could have escaped being fined for any length of time and no such fine is recorded under the name of Maggie *Gillon*. The name "Maggie" was popular in the later half of the 1800's—eleven sporting ladies bearing "Maggie" as their first names are listed in the Wichita police records from 1873 through 1875. The names Maggie *Hedges* and Maggie *Reed* (also recorded as *Reid*) show up several times in the Wichita police dockets prior to 1875 as being fined for prostitution along with Bessie and Sallie Earp. It is not out of the range of plausibility to suggest that she could very well have used either, or even both, "Hedges" and "Reed" as aliases prior to adopting "Wood" as her surname. It seems a highly unlikely coincidence that of all the prostitutes listed in the Wichita police records, the name "Maggie" would appear regularly with the Earp ladies.

The first mention of her as Maggie *Wood* is in the afore-mentioned 1875 census. Rather than an amorous relationship,

Maggie may have first taken George's surname because it was a common practice for the girls to take the name of their pimps. However, in general, the couple seems to have been regarded as a common law man and wife. It was not until December 9, 1879, that "George B. Wood, Sedgwick County, Kansas, age 25" and "Maggie Gillon, Sedgwick County, Kansas, age 22," applied for a marriage license and did in fact, make their marriage legal on that date.[6]

Wichita police records show Bessie and Sallie Earp to be in business in Wichita from January, 1874 until some time in March of 1875. March happened to be the month when the 1875 census was taken which listed female "Geo" (taken to be Maggie) as head of that household. In consideration of the foregoing, it does seem likely that Maggie may have taken over Bessie Earp's "house" sometime in March of 1875.

Drago, in *Notorious Ladies of the Frontier* states, "The toughest dive on Water Street was conducted by Mag Woods. She was arrested innumerable times and fined for conducting a disorderly house. Her husband, George Woods, an unsavory saloon character and two-bit gambler, ran her errands and did her bidding. Mag [was] coarse, pugnacious, hard as nails."[7] This statement, while enhancing the picture somewhat, can for the most part, be confirmed by information found in Wichita police records.

2

In May of the next year (1876), young Charles Francis Colcord, with his father struck out from deep in southern Texas with 1200 horses headed for the Chisholm Trail to Kansas. In his autobiography, he relates that when they passed Fort Worth, Maggie had, "brought a lot of corn fed girls down from Kansas and they were going to have a big party at Fort Worth." Colcord continued:

> I will never forget Mag Woods' dance hall. They were just building this big shack. The floor was completed, the roof and part of the siding was on and where the siding was lacking the holes were stopped up with wagon sheets and canvas. At one end there was a rough bar with five bartenders, all as busy as could be. There was a motley crowd in this dance hall. Mag had about thirty girls that she had brought from Wichita, Kansas. She charged fifty cents a set for dancing and it was a sight to see those old buffalo hunters, cowpunchers and railroad men swing those girls. About midnight, after the whiskey had been flowing very freely, a gunfight developed. The lights were shot out, one or two men were killed and several were badly hurt. Places like that dance hall took a fellow's money right away from him.[8]

Nothing else is known of Maggie's Texas excursion. Colcord's is the only reference found relating to this "party". Nothing was found in the Fort Worth or Dallas newspapers of the time so it is not known if George made the trip with Maggie (and perhaps was responsible for erecting the "shack".) An excerpt from Anne Seagraves' book, *Soiled Doves* offers one plausible explanation of the affair:

> A few of the madams would occasionally take their girls on what was referred to as a "summer vacation." They would set up large tents near, or within, a mining camp or town, and the ladies would go to work. The miners were delighted and it increased business. It also provided the girls with a change of scenery. When they returned to their brothels in the city, it was often with renewed energy. Madams like these were well liked by their girls.[9]

By September of 1876, Maggie was back to her old tricks and doing business as usual in Wichita where she was fined as a prostitute five times and ten times as a madam. George was fined several times for "miscellaneous" and interestingly; the record shows that he, himself, was fined as a "keeper of a house of ill fame" in March of 1878.[10] In September of 1875, George purchased Lot #44 on Wichita Street, (Munger's Addition). An 1878 Wichita City Directory lists him as a "contractor" living on the corner of Wichita Street and 1st.[11]

A picture emerges of George as an opportunistic street hustler and pimp in his young Wichita days. He stands out in one notorious bit of Wichita history: He once stood off officers on the Douglas Avenue Bridge in October 1876, and buffaloed Deputy Massey with his six-shooter.[12] It has been suggested that it was this incident that Wyatt Earp borrowed to portray *himself* as the hero in his telling of a similar fictitious showdown with a gang of bloodthirsty Texans on this same famous bridge across the Arkansas River.

In Stuart Lake's widely read Wyatt Earp biography, Lake records anecdotes related by Earp. Many of Earp's stories are generally regarded as being self-aggrandizing and largely composed of half-true or stretched tales fabricated or built upon from various incidents that he may or may not have been involved in. In 1959, ninety-three year old Wichita native, Captain Sam Jones, was asked in an interview: "Captain, did Wyatt Earp tame Wichita?" The Captain replied, "If anybody cleaned up Wichita it was Mike Meagher. Wyatt was just a policeman. I used to see him every day....My grandmother was the cook in Bessie Earp's whorehouse."[13]

It is apparent that George and Wyatt rubbed shoulders in Wichita and no doubt Earp made several of the arrests that resulted in the fines that Maggie had to pay requisite to conducting business. Michael Meagher, Marshal of Wichita at this time, was another famous lawman who dealt with George and likely hauled Maggie into Wichita's police court more than once.

Mike Meagher is venerated in Wichita, the Sedgwick County Seat, as one of the "Four Horsemen" who secured Wichita's future as a cattle-shipping point. He was twice Marshal of Wichita and was at one time a U.S. Deputy Marshal. His twin brother, John, was at times his deputy and Sedgwick

County Sheriff. Wyatt Earp worked for Mike Meagher as a policeman. After a fight with a fellow officer and an incident in which he was suspected of embezzling city fine monies that he had collected from prostitutes, Earp's reputation became clouded and Meagher fired him. He fell from grace and soon left Wichita.

Mike and John Meagher

On New Year's Eve, 1876, Marshal Meagher collared a celebrating stage coach driver named Sylvester Powell for assault and put him behind bars. Powell's incarceration didn't cool his hostility—immediately upon his release from jail, he went gunning for the Marshal. Meagher happened to be in the outhouse at the rear of Mayor Hope's saloon when shots burned through the door. With a gunshot wound in his leg, Meagher charged out of the privy to engage his nemesis hand-to-hand.

He met Powell in storm of gunfire taking another bullet through his hand in the fray. After a brief skirmish and a single shot from Meagher's pistol, Sylvester Powell lay dead.

Meagher was exonerated of any wrongdoing but the incident may have been the cause of his undoing—yet to come.

3

In mid 1879, and in anticipation of the railroad's entry into Caldwell and the coming year's cattle trade, it was Caldwell's turn to boom.

> Talk about Caldwell "booming;" she has never realized what "booming" was till the past two weeks. When it comes to one land agent, alone, making forty-one deeds, in one day to settlers, regardless of speculators, we can then begin to realize that she is soon to be the "metropolis of the south-west." Men of capital and influence are seen on our streets daily, and men who are buying property to become permanent settlers. The buildings that have [gone] up since our last issue is astonishing. Carpenters are coming in almost every day, and still they can't do half the work that is to be done.[14]

While great optimistic fervor permeated the business community concerning the commercial aspects of the boom, the city of Caldwell had the benefit of knowledge of the experiences that its predecessors had had and could foresee trouble looming ahead. In an expedient effort to mitigate what was viewed as a necessary evil, the Caldwell city council passed an ordinance relating to offenses against chastity, morality and decency. But, with many other enterprising newcomers, George and Maggie Wood shared the promise of prosperity in the bright future of Caldwell. By September 1879, shortly before her marriage, Maggie was doing business in temporary quarters at Caldwell, scouting the locale and gleaning intelligence for the assault that she and George would make upon the city.

The September 4th Caldwell *Post* forebode: "Mag Woods, a notorious Wichita prostitute, in company with several pieces of feminine frailty, made a descent from that unchristian city on our little village last week, and temporarily located on the creek, outside the city limits."[15] In October the *Post* continued, "Several ladies of easy virtue now reside in Caldwell—so we are informed."[16]

Nevertheless, public optimism was rampant and on December 31, 1879, the township unanimously voted for the railroad bond that would bring the rails into Caldwell.

Proud of its progress since its meager beginnings a decade earlier, the *Post* reviewed the short recent history of the boom:

> This was the opening of a new era for our place, for as soon as it became known that the [rail] road would terminate at Caldwell, prosperity commenced to set in. Town lots began to rise and assume considerable dignity and surrounding farms were transformed into "additions to Caldwell."…The city of Caldwell, having become incorporated during the month of July, 1879, kindly enclosed all the surrounding additions and "took them in." The city has one of the finest town sites in Kansas. It soon became a certainty that Caldwell would be the shipping point for a large amount of cattle…and that the Railroad Company contemplated to build extensive cattle yards here. This fact becoming generally known, soon resulted

in a large addition to our population. Houses sprang up on every side; our stores became filled with goods and our streets with people. In the mean time the railroad kept coming nearer and nearer, and its approach was eagerly watched by the citizens of our burgh. All knew that its advent would bring with it a material increase in population, trade and prosperity...Persons knowing whereof they speak, declare that Caldwell will have the finest stock yards of all now owned by the railroad company. Besides the many advantages which Caldwell will reap from being a cattle market, the fact of being the terminus of the road makes it a distributing point for a vast amount of government supplies which will be shipped to this place to be hauled from here to the different posts and agencies in the [Indian] territory...[17]

George and Maggie were consumed in the intense excitement of this promising atmosphere. They were well schooled in all the sordid gambits; cons, schemes and angles employed in catering to man's immoral instincts. Captivated by the prospect of easy money, they intently formulated their plans and brazenly laid the groundwork for the creation of the Red Light Saloon.

Amid a myriad of fortune seekers, Mike Meagher, too, could foresee the coming boom and in 1879 left Wichita for Caldwell where he opened the Arcade Saloon. In April of 1880, soon after arriving in Caldwell, Meagher became that city's third mayor and also served as Caldwell's City Marshal for a brief period.

As mayor, Meagher again found himself concerned with Maggie's antics as he had been in Wichita. On May 1st the city caught up with Maggie for the first of many times—she was hauled in for being "drunk and disorderly," an indulgence that she joyfully repeated regularly. At the same time, it was found necessary to fine her for "running a house of ill fame."[18]

Maggie had operated in Caldwell about six months before George obtained real estate, the first phase of their plan. On March 25th of 1880, George purchased Lot #118, Chisholm Street, Original Town of Caldwell. There they commenced the establishment of the Red Light Saloon.

George bought the property from John H. Wendell (also shown as "Wendels" in some references). Wendell was proprietor of the City Hotel, also known as the Caldwell House, and a livery stable keeper as well as a part time real estate man. Wendell incidentally, in September of 1879 was the first arrest recorded in Caldwell's first police docket book. His offense was riding his horse too fast in the town and was the cause of the first arrest made by Caldwell's first marshal, Marshal George Flatt.

Wendell had purchased lot #118 from Henry R. Turnbaugh for twenty dollars, which gave him possession of nearly the entire block. He then sold the lot to George Wood less than one month later for $125. The adjoining Lot #116 was annexed to the Red Light property by virtue of a tax deed sometime later.

Over the years, there has been much speculation as to the location of the old Red Light Saloon—at least four different locations have been cited in various books. What was known as Lot #118 Chisholm Street in the early days of Caldwell is now known to be the northeast corner of Central (east Highway 81) and Chisholm Streets—one block east of Caldwell's Main Street and one block west of the old Chisholm Trail thoroughfare where it passed through the city[19]

Deed to the Red Light Property

Circumstances as to how the Red Light building came to be erected are in question due to a story the *Post* carried on April 22nd of 1880. The story has caused some confusion and uncertainty:

> George Wood's two story building has been removed from Wichita to Caldwell. It is being erected, we presume for convenience sake, near the calaboose. If this building is built for the purpose of a dance house, we hope the mayor will keep the building on the move.[20]

Following one week later:

> Three men working on the two-story building located
> near the calaboose fell off the roof last Monday afternoon.
> Two of them were quite severely injured.[21]

It has been questioned whether the actual two-story *building* was moved from Wichita to Caldwell—or only the *business* was moved.

In *Cattle Towns*, Dykstra reports, "Caldwell received its one and only dance house in 1880, when, the railroad tracks having just entered town, a notorious Wichita couple, George and Margaret Woods, unloaded a two-story bagnio from a flatcar and saw to its reconstitution there."[22] Dykstra quotes the *Post* story above as his source and apparently presupposes that the Red Light building was conveyed to Caldwell by rail.

While that would seem to be a fair assumption, it should be considered that flatcars of that era were about seven feet wide and twenty-two to twenty-four feet long—not capable of hauling a very large structure. Moreover, Wood was issued a dram-shop license in early May and the Red Light most likely opened on Saturday, May 15, 1880, or perhaps, several days before.[23] Also, it is known that the Cowley, Sumner & Ft. Worth tracks (a Santa Fe development company) did not enter Caldwell until several weeks later on June 1st so it appears evident that the building could not have been transported by rail.[24]

While possible, it would seem extremely unlikely that a structure of the size that the Red Light must have been, could have been moved the 60 plus miles overland from Wichita to Caldwell by any sort of horse-drawn tandem wagon arrangement unless, perhaps, it was dismantled into multiple small manageable units, moved and then reassembled. However, Wood is listed in the 1875 census as "laborer" and in the Wichita City Directory of 1878 as a "contractor" so, in addition to his other activities, he may have had the skills necessary to manage such a complex undertaking.

In any event, the Red Light came to be, and as it opened, the *Post* expressed the sentiment of many of the townspeople in a vain attempt to dissuade the city from allowing the existence of the dance house.

> In every frontier town wherein money promises to be plenty, there springs up a certain nuisance, to put as mildly as one can, namely, the dance-house. It is the hot-bed of vice and the favorite place for murders, assault and drunken ribaldry. A gambling room is as moral as a church raffle, and a saloon as quiet as a funeral, when compared with the dance-house. If you want the revolver cracking and the bullet doing its deadly work in your midst; if you want to have the most degrading men and women making night hideous with their hellish orgies; if you want to pollute the air which your wives and mothers breath; just tolerate a dance house in your midst.[25]

The plea was to no avail and a week later the *Post* published another letter:

Editor Caldwell Post:

DEAR SIR: Knowing the detriment that a "Dance House" would be to Caldwell, if allowed in our city, the writer of this article visited the "Red Light saloon" last Saturday night. The scenes there presented reminded me of the early times in Cheyenne, when murder ran riot and the pistol was the only argument. It is true that the assemblage was sober, orderly and quiet Saturday night—but we must remember that it was composed chiefly of men who visited the place merely out of curiosity. Then again, it is a new thing, and has not as yet accumulated the crowd of pimps, hangers-on and deadbeats, who generally make such a place their headquarters. It is a well-known fact—as any Western man can testify to—that the greatest curse frontier towns have ever had, has been the so-called "dance houses" or "hurdy-gurdies." The lowest, both male and female, congregate at these places: the vilest of liquors are there dealt out, and everything is done that will bring the worst passions of mankind into action. In fact, the class of persons who run "dance houses" are such as a respectable sportsman and gambler would not associate with. The femalese as a rule, have some "lowdown" male, as a lover, who is too lazy to work and too much of a coward to be anything but a "sneak-thief," who depends upon the wages of their shame for a livelihood, and urge these female friends on to commit crimes which they would not do otherwise. In fact, a "dance-house" if permitted to exist in our midst, will bring to our city a class of cut-throats, thieves, etc., which we do not desire, and for this, if no other reason, the city authorities should at once take measures to close all such places. (signed) CALDWELL[26]

In spite of its unwelcome entry into the Caldwell business community, the Red Light prevailed. In effect, the article conceded that the Red Light had emerged victorious in its struggle. In the same issue is found the first of many complaints that followed: "Stop that 'dance house' racket".[27]

Amazingly, the young couple had succeeded—the Red Light flourished. George was 26 and Maggie was 22.

4

Caldwell businesses thrived; the town burgeoned and became known far and wide as "The Queen of the Border."

In an article in the Caldwell *Messenger*, Grant Harris, early day printer at the Caldwell *Post* states, "Caldwell's saloons, dance halls, and gambling houses did more business than those at Abilene. With only 500 population, Caldwell had six or seven saloons [actually fourteen saloons of record], each with a gambling house in connection and the largest dance hall in Kansas—the Red Light."[28]

> The house was a two-story building; the front was furnished as a saloon, of which George Woods was the Proprietor. Upon the front window the following words "Red Light Saloon" were inscribed. Mag Woods, the notorious woman known as Wood's wife, was the proprietress of the dance hall, which was run in connection with the saloon. Wichita lent her worst inmates to become inmates of this hall, and part of the population of Caldwell.[29]

At least nineteen of the 133 known prostitutes found in the early Caldwell police docket books appear to have had association with Maggie at different times throughout her sojourn in the Border Queen. It seems to be a virtual certainty that there were many more whose connection with Maggie can not now be established. It is not known how many of these girls worked at the Red Light at a given time. Freeman, discussing the Red Light in *Midnight and Noonday* says that Maggie: "with 10 or 12 prostitutes, made it their abiding place."[30] An interesting insight into the question is George's probate asset inventory that lists 7 beds, 7 wash stands, 7 mirrors in addition to he and Maggie's personal furniture that was listed separately.[31]

Another indication of the size of their operation can be found in the 1880 Census that lists those connected with the Red Light as:

> George B. Wood, White, 27, Married, Dance House/ Saloon Keeper
> Maggie Wood, White, 23, Married, Wife, Keeping House
> Becky Banks, Black, 24, Single, Servant, Cook
> Wash Walker, White, 25, Single, Boarder, Keeping Bar
> William Dexter, White, 25, Married, Boarder, Works in house
> Lizzie Roberts, White, 20, Single, Boarder, Dancing
> Mary Balize(?), White, 17, Single, Boarder, Dancing
> Belle Piper, White, 27, Married, Boarder, Dancing
> Lucy Moody, White, 18, Single, Boarder, Dancing
> George Brower(?), White, 6, Boarder [Son of Belle Piper?]
> Charles Hardy, White, 21, Single, Servant, Bar Keeper
> Harry Cabdeu(?), White, 34, Single, Boarder, Occupation illegible
> George Reed, White, 23, Single, Boarder, No Occupation

All of the females listed have numerous arrests recorded in connection with prostitution—the four dancers as "inmates of houses of ill fame" and Becky Banks and Maggie, of course, each as "keepers of houses of ill fame."

Before becoming employed as cook at the Red Light, Rebecca Banks was one of the first madams arrested in Caldwell. She was inexplicably fined $50—the harshest fine ever imposed for any offense by the contemporary Caldwell Police Court—five times the normal $10 fine imposed upon "keepers". It may have been a discriminatory gesture, as Becky happened to be a black madam. The fine may have been what caused the downfall of her former "business" and the impetus that led her to the Red Light's kitchen.

◆   ◆   ◆

It is not known which or how many of those listed actually resided *in* the Red Light. If all of them did, then a logical deduction would indicate that a minimum of eight bedrooms would surely have been required. In that case, only four of the rooms would have been allocated as private rooms for the use of the working girls. It is difficult to imagine the Red Light's rise to such prominence with only four girls in service and is almost certainly not the case. The surprising inclusion of only four doves, politely shown as "Dancing" in the census, immediately leads to the speculative conclusion that the Red Light must have housed many more rooms. How many is anyone's guess. The deduction from that line of contemplation would indicate that the Red Light must have been a substantially large building.

There is a likelihood that another residence may have been employed to provide additional private rooms for the girls and/or for the gentlemen listed. It is also possible, if not probable, that George and Maggie may have preferred a domicile other than the Red Light.

A composite of nefarious operations similar to Maggie's presents a scenario likely to be fairly representative of how she might have managed her female retinue. In addition to her "in house" girls, there were probably many "independents" or freelance "dancers" with whom Maggie had a working understanding. Such a girl would be allowed to dance in the Red Light for a fee that her cowboy partner paid to the house. After the dance, she would charm her mark into buying them both drinks (hers, greatly watered down of course). She would then be paid a percentage of the dance fee and would retain a portion or perhaps all of the tip. In return, the house benefited from its percentage of the dance fees and the proceeds from the considerably over-priced drinks.

The young lady would entice the cowboy into buying as many drinks and rounds of dancing as possible—all the while encouraging a further "business" relationship. If an intimate engagement was agreed upon, the couple might retreat "upstairs" to one of the Red Light rooms or they might leave the hall and go the girl's residence, or perhaps to the cowboy's hotel room. In either case, the girl was sure to pay Maggie the percentage due lest she expose herself to the pain of George's wrath. Such a foolish girl would never work in Caldwell again.

◆   ◆   ◆

Maggie was the first Madam to be arrested in Caldwell. Seemingly a perpetual party girl, she is exposed in the police records as being boisterous to the extreme. Fisticuffs seem to have been as common between the Red Light women as it was among the cowboys and Maggie's impetuous disposition suggests that she was probably the cause of most of them. Exuding a tempestuous spirit, she was irrepressible—her unrestrained carousing and fighting landed her in Judge Kelly's court a number of times along with several of her sorority.

George's roguish nature also shows up in the Caldwell police docket books. He was arrested three times by lawman Frank Hunt for riding his horse on the sidewalk, for carrying a concealed weapon, and for assault and battery.[32]

The infamy and disrepute that the Woods and the Red Light propagated was in no way undeserved. The nature of the attractions that they provided appealed mightily to the coarser pent-up instincts of their patrons. To be sure, men of the neighboring towns who preferred not to be seen philandering in their own communities visited the Red Light. More likely to be found in the den were transient cavalry soldiers and the railroaders that manned the cattle trains that ran day and night throughout the shipping season.

Cowpunchers punching cows: Derivation of the term
"Cowpuncher"
Photo courtesy of Gloria White

But by far, most of the Red Light's patrons were the cowboys; either fresh from the trail or in town from the surrounding ranches. Many of the later had endured months of lonely isolation on remote ranches, far removed from any civilization.

When those cowboys finally got into town, the combination of money in their pockets and whiskey in their bellies invariably led to outrageous, many times violent, actions committed upon the streets of Caldwell.

For several years the drunken cowboys would "take the town" at their pleasure…The general consequences of such proceedings was that the cowboy would commit some serious offense while under the influence of whiskey and would either leave town with the marshal in pursuit of him, or he would be tried and fined ten, twenty, or twenty-five dollars. His companions would generally come to his rescue, pay his fine, and after he was released, the cowboy, together with his friends, would get the drop on the marshal, and to use the phrase familiar in the wild west, would "take the town." "Taking the town" usually consisted in riding up and down the streets; shooting at sign boards, at the glass window fronts of the stores; ordering whiskey at the muzzle of the six shooter; riding their horses on the pavements and hotel verandahs; and, in fact they were at liberty to run things their own way. Sometimes the citizens would arm themselves and attempt to quiet the "boys", and generally a riot would ensue, a pitch battle would take place, oftentimes ending in bloodshed.[33]

Six months after the Red Light had opened, the *Post* jested:

There have been but two fights in town this week. Now, the next fellow who says we are not getting civilized down here is liable to get hurt.[34]

It was not an uncommon sight to see the women of ill-repute parading the streets, mingling with the innocent girls of the town and vicinity and luring many unfortunate victims to the Red Light, where they were either robbed and pitched into the streets or squandered their money while under the influence of their vile whiskey, only to "sober up" and find they were "busted." Then their hatred for the place is being manifested in various ways; they begin to shoot at sign boards, ride up and down the street firing off their revolvers promiscously, and the final result is, either the death of the offenders or an officer is shot down while in discharge of his duties.

The Red Light was notorious throughout the west; Wichita lent her worst characters to become its inmates. The house and inmates is said to have accomplished the ruin of several of Caldwell's brightest young girls...."

Cowboys...meet with companions of former acquaintance, visit the various saloons and gambling holes,...loose the larger proportion of their money, then as a last resort, visit the houses of ill fame and lose their remaining "little all."...the air is filled with the echo of their lewd songs...the night is passed in debauchery and delights such as the "Red Light."[35]

The mindset of those young men is well illustrated by a man who, as one of those young cowboys, frequented Caldwell in that era. In his autobiography, he relates some of his exploits as a brash young cowboy and provides unusually vivid insights into the motivations and mentality of the cowboys that patronized the Red Light Saloon. Several of these are included below.

I got into an altercation with the bartender over something which I have forgotten and hard words came quickly. As he passed in front of me I reached over the bar and grabbed him by the shoulder in order to pull him across the bar and whip him. His shirt gave way in my hand, so he jerked loose from me and reached for his gun which was lying on top of the bar. As he took hold of his gun, before he could raise it I shot through his hand, knocking the gun from his hand and sending it spinning down the bar…. But most of the men I knew at that time would have killed him when he reached for that gun…he certainly would have shot me if I hadn't shot first…(He went) to a hospital in Wichita where I paid his expenses. That was all that was ever done about it.

Riding a stampede is the most thrilling experience a man could have; one seems to feel just as wild as the steers or horses do. I would rather ride a stampede than do anything else on earth. It is impossible to describe the feeling it produces.

…McCartney had the rope around his hips to keep it from burning his hands, but the mare came out with such a terrible rush that it jerked him off his feet and he fell flat, face down in the dust, with the mare and the rope gone. Of course everybody was laughing. When he got up he was the angriest man you ever saw. He grabbed a broken bar from the gate four or five feet long and rushed at me. I saw that he was enraged! I waited until he got almost up to me, then drew my six-shooter and fired, but as I leveled my gun, Bill Fawcett [Fosset] ran between us and knocked my gun up and took the bullet in his hand. McCartney stopped right there and quieted down-though he was a very bad and dangerous man. Fawcett has the mark of that bullet on his hand today. Later he became marshal of Kingman, Kansas. (Fosset also served as an Assistant Marshal of Caldwell and had an active role in the "Talbot Raid," covered in Chapter 9.)

...and in accordance with cowboy custom began riding our horses at a run up and down the main street of the town. We'd had some drinks, of course but all of us were sober enough not to shoot anybody. However, two or three of the boys had been doing a little shooting earlier in the day and evidently the patience of the town was exhausted, for as we lined up for our last run down the street, going back to the range, the city marshal got out in the street and headed us off. I happened to be nearest so he reached for my horse as we rode up, grabbing the left side of my horse's bit with his left hand. I swung at him with my gun, reaching over my horse's neck, but the blow fell short and he pulled down with his gun, jabbing it against my breast solidly and snapped it. It failed to fire and he did the same thing again, and again the gun failed to fire. By that time the rest of the boys had closed in and one of them struck the marshal on the head with his Winchester...[we] eventually made our peace with the marshal...Nothing was ever said about it and we were all good friends afterward...just...an example of a type of a thing that happened over and over when the cowboys were in town. They were easy to anger, quick to act and very dangerous in action. Only men of that type and nerve were able to prevail over conditions which surrounded them from day to day.

The Indians had cut...leaving the bodies of our two boys in the wagon bed where they had fallen. I pulled four arrows out of Bristow's heart, shot in from the right side under the arm, and I drew three or four out of Fred's body.

I looked him in the eye and rolled over two or three times, got up and shot his head off with my six-shooter. It made my blood run cold when I got a good look at him. He was a big timber rattlesnake and had seventeen rattles, much larger and more deadly than the prairie rattlers.

I was riding at full speed when a yearling suddenly dropped back out of the herd. My horse hit it, turned a complete somersault and fell with me under him...I thought I was dead...It was a long time before I could ride again. I had a terrible cough that lasted for several years...My left side is still caved in from that fall.

Although I look back and recall all the things we did to break the monotony of our existence, it was still a hard and lonely life; rough and violent most of the time. Those who read about the old days and the rough manner in which the boys had their "good times" when they got into towns or other civilized places, would find it easier to understand if they would stop and think of the weeks and months that these young, active men spent in lonely solitude; in constant contact with the most violent forces of nature; drenched by the rains and buffeted by the winds and storms; having to deal continuously with the cussedness of half wild cattle; with wild animals and wilder Indians, the whole of which almost completely made up our daily lives. When we were off duty with money to spend our relief often just naturally took violent form, consonant with the life we lived every day. One's most constant companion was his gun. He wore it everywhere—almost slept with it. It was perfectly natural that the gun retained its essential place when we were on our "outings". As I recall some of the things we did under circumstances of that day and time I realize how we must have shocked the quiet, sober people of the towns to which we went for our "outings". How foreign my attitude then—to my outlook of today. Yes, today it is easy for me to understand that our actions then were the natural outgrowth of the life we lived. It was just as natural in those days for us to go in and shoot up a town and raise hell generally as it is nowadays to go to see a football game or play a game of golf, and there was no more evil intent then than there is in these relaxations of today.

I suppose I was no better and no worse than the other fellows of my age who rode the range with me. As I think back over it I am certainly not proud of them; neither can I say that I am ashamed, for it was an essential part of the life, the place and the times...[36]

Incredulously, the young cowboy of these accounts was later to become one of the foremost citizens of the State of Oklahoma. He became the first Police Chief then first City Marshal of Oklahoma City, then a U. S. Marshal and Sheriff of Oklahoma County. He went on to become one of the most respected figures of Oklahoma City in the 1920's as a bank president, Hotel builder, and leader in the real estate and oil business.

5

On September 9, 1880 the Caldwell *Post* reported:

> Last Thursday afternoon the city had a light shooting scrape. It seems that one W. F. Smith, a herder—had liquored up pretty freely, so that the ordinances of the quiet city of Caldwell became a myth—and the police even entirely forgotten. He rode around the town now and then flourishing his revolver, believing no doubt he was lord of all he surveyed. Of course he struck the "Red-Light"—they all do it. Then he commenced firing a salute...Policeman [Frank] Hunt met him...and ordered him to halt. In reply he drew his revolver, when Frank elevated his shot gun and lodged a buck shot in Mr. Smith's knee, and [killed] his horse. A great deal of sympathy was expressed for the horse...

About a month later, the readers of the October 14, 1880 *Post* were once again informed of "another man for breakfast!" The story reported that lawman Frank Hunt had been murdered in the Red Light Saloon.

ANOTHER MURDER

Last Friday evening [October 8], this city was again thrown into an excitement over another murder. About ten o'clock some cowardly assassin shot Frank Hunt and inflicted, what afterwards proved a fatal wound. Hunt was down at that den of iniquity, the Red Light dance house, and while sitting at the north window in the dance hall, someone shot him, the ball entering his body on the left side, passing over and fracturing the tenth rib and lodging in the ninth costal cartilage on the right side. The shot was fired through the open window, by some person standing outside. Who that person was, is only a matter or rumor and suspicion.... Shortly after the death of Frank Hunt, David Spear of this town, was arrested under a warrant from Justice Kelly, and is still held in custody.

The *Post* again loudly voiced its condemnation:

We cannot refrain from saying that it is our opinion that if the Council had listened to our protestations against the running of the "dance house," this murder would not have happened in our place. The POST again and again lifted up its voice against it, and calling to mind what like dens have done for other cities. Our words have proved true, and we charge the Council with being blamable for these shameful, horrid happenings in our midst. Both the murders of Flatt and of Hunt goes straight back to the Red Light Dance house.[37]

The suspected perpetrator, 17 year old David Spear, was the younger of two brothers who figure prominently in the Red Light saga.

The Spear family was notorious in Caldwell and seemed always to be at the center of trouble. Patriarch Charles L. Spear, proprietor of the IXL Saloon, was walking along side of

Caldwell's ex-marshal George Flat when the latter was shot down in a fusillade in the middle of Caldwell's Main Street. The elder Spear was later suspected of complicity in the ambush by a shadowy coteire. George Spear, the older of Charles' two unprincipled sons, plays a significant part in the story yet to come.

The next November, in the wake of Hunt's murder, a policeman was stationed at the Red Light on a full time basis. He was paid by the Red Light but had full police authority under the city Marshal. He was George Reed, the person listed as "boarder" at the Red Light in the 1880 census. He appears to have done odd jobs around the place and may have sometimes functioned as a bouncer. He is listed as a witness in several murder trials emanating from the Red Light and was the occasional driver of George's Hunnewell coach service.

◆   ◆   ◆

The couple continued to prosper. On February 16, 1881, George and Maggie invested $100 in Lot #22 of Block #33 in a new town ten or eleven miles to the east of Caldwell called Hunnewell. The Santa Fe tracks ran from north to south through the middle of the site, bisecting it east from west. The center of activity was along a street called "Smoky Row" that paralleled the east side of the tracks. (Sometimes also called "Front Street," it was actually *Sixth* Street.) There, two blocks north of the cattle pens, on the corner of Oak Street and Smoky Row, they built a saloon/dancehall/brothel auxiliary to the Caldwell Red Light—they named it appropriately, "The Red Light Saloon."

Shortly after, George provided a means of transportation for anyone wanting to patronize the place:

> As will be seen by advertisement in another column, Geo. B. Wood has established a daily line of stages between Caldwell and Hunnewell. He has put the price down to 50 cents each way or $1.00 for the round trip and will run every day, leaving the Leland Hotel in Caldwell punctually at 9 o'clock a.m., passengers or no passengers. Mr. Wood has the best of teams, a careful and accommodating driver, and will do his full share to merit the patronage of those whose business or pleasure requires them to travel from one place to the other.[38]

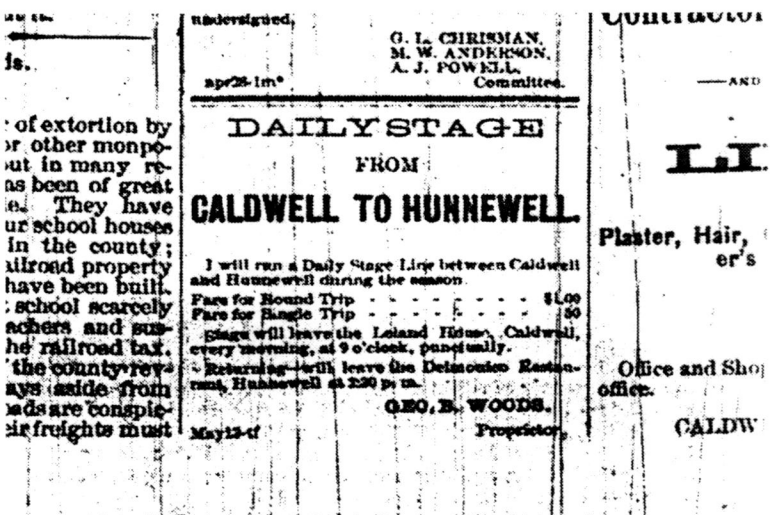

Wood's Advertisement

The early Hunnewell newspapers have not been photographed for microfilm and copies of that era are not known to exist. Therefore, very few records of events at the Hunnewell Red Light have survived.

6

An article in the Caldwell *Post* on September 30, 1880 announced, "Fred Kuhlman, the pioneer cowboy, has purchased the Kentucky Saloon on the corner of Main and Fifth streets, where he will keep a full assortment of Liquors, Kentucky Sour Mash Whiskey, Cigars, Etc. A first class pool table in connection. Fred is a jolly good fellow and will hold a good hand with the boys." A good fellow indeed—he was arrested and fined two weeks after the article appeared for disturbing the peace and for carrying a revolver. Five days later he was fined again for running a poker game in his saloon.

It is apparent that George and Fred were very close friends and that George, being the better businessman, occasionally lent Fred money and helped him in his business dealings. On May 11, 1881, George accommodated Fred with an incomprehensibly contorted business arrangement wherein Fred would acquire one half interest in the Woods' Red Light at Hunnewell for $450 which he would pay back to George over time.[39] Kuhlman then managed the Hunnewell Red Light only one month when, on June 23, in front of the Red Light, he was shot and killed in an altercation over Miss Mattie Smith, one of Maggie's Caldwell Red Light girls who had gone to work at the Hunnewell Red Light and became Kuhlman's current aficionada. Mattie had logged 4 arrests in Caldwell for prostitution.

MURDER AT HUNNEWELL

Fred Kuhlman, a former resident of this place [Caldwell], was shot and killed at Hunnewell last Thursday morning by a man named Ed. Stokley, boss herder for Forsythe. The cause of the shooting was a woman, and a prostitute of course. The parties had some difficulty about the creature the night previous. On Thursday morning the two men met on the street, when Stokley pulled his revolver and fired at Kuhlman, shooting him in the right breast, the ball passing entirely through his body and coming out near the backbone.

The Hunnewell *Independent* says says that after the shooting, Stokley walked up to his victim, looked at him, then stepped back a few yards and reloaded his revolver, held it up, saying, "this is what did it," and went into Ford's store, bought some cartridges and a twenty-six shot Winchester rifle, paid his bill, got on his horse and left for the Territory before any attempt was made to arrest him. The marshal was out of the city at the time. Everyone seemed horrified at the deed and could do nothing.

Kuhlman died about thirty minutes after he was shot, and was brought over and buried in the cemetery at this place.

So far as we can learn no efforts have been made to arrest Stokley, and it is likely that he will go on killing men who happen to displease him in any way until finally some one quicker with a gun than he is, puts an end to his murderous career.[40]

Kuhlman died deeply in debt to George. In the end George paid for his funeral, his coffin and the suit of clothes that he was buried in.

7

After the murder of Fred Kuhlman, George went to Hunnewell to assume management of the Red Light there while Maggie was left to "dispense sweetness" in Caldwell. They took on a man named James "Big Jim" Cavner to help Maggie manage the Red Light in Caldwell. About a month later on August 1st, Maggie, Big Jim, and Lizzie Roberts, a 20 year-old dove of Maggie's flock, went on an excursion to visit George at Hunnewell.

Hunnewell had a newly appointed Marshal. Joseph Dolan, himself having been arrested in Caldwell in early 1880 for "disturbing the peace and quietude," had been Caldwell's Assistant Marshal before becoming the Hunnewell City Marshal only days before. Previously in Caldwell, Lizzie Roberts had been arrested half a dozen times for various offenses including prostitution and for being drunk, and disorderly. Maggie and Lizzie appear to have been close friends—several of their wild parties in Caldwell had resulted in their arrest and Dolan had been the arresting officer in one of these adventures.

When the clique convened in the Hunnewell Red Light, the inevitable party ensued and, predictably, troubles followed.

The *Commercial* reported:

...Cavner was full of whisky, got into quarrel with some one and seizing an empty Winchester waltzed through the town making everybody stand around to suit him. He was finally arrested [apparently by Marshal Dolan] and taken before the Police Judge with his gun in his hand. The Judge told him he must put that implement away, and Jim set it outside of the door. The judge then fined Jim $21 for his little bit of amusement. This incensed his royal highness, and reaching behind him, he picked up the Winchester, which one of the women had loaded and placed at his back, [and] told the Judge to go to a supposed hot place and left.[41]

As can best be surmised, the party continued with Cavner being the most troublesome of the four prompting Marshal Dolan to attempt to arrest him again. Cavner, already enraged by Dolan's earlier interference in his festivities, resisted his arrest and a major scuffle followed. Maggie and Lizzie Roberts, perhaps harboring some residual animosity from their earlier encounters with Dolan, came to Cavner's aid. George, too, dove in even though; two days before the murder of Fred Kuhlman, in an obviously friendly transaction, George had lent then Caldwell Deputy Marshal Dolan $205. Dolan had signed a note dated June 21, 1881, drawing ten-percent interest and due in ninety days. The friendship counted for naught—needless to say, Marshal Dolan was the looser of the lop-sided battle and later:

...The entire party came over to Caldwell that night or Sunday morning. Meantime the Police Judge went up to Wellington and swore out a warrant for their arrest, and on Monday Sheriff Thralls came down, arrested the mob and took them up to the county seat. [42]

As spelled out *in Case #113—The State of Kansas vs. Geo. B. Wood, et al,* the foursome "did strike, pummel, and severely beat Joseph Dolan."

In their defense, the four culprits retained Caldwell attorney, Samuel Berry, himself with an extensive police record in Caldwell. The trial was held in Wellington, the Sumner County Seat, and in the court records of that case can be found a legal brief consisting of a poem that Counselor Berry had written to Judge Ike N. King, apparently lamenting a hangover that resulted from a night of carousing in Wellington with his four clients the previous night:

> APOSTROPHE TO THE COURT
> I hope you'll decide to my liking
>   For I'm sleepy and tired
>   And I want to be fired
>   Out of court (for a spell)
>   Over prairie and dell
>   Over morass and fell
>   Till I light in Caldwell
>   In the Leland Hotel
> And sleep forty winks without waking
> Oh, Ike King
> Oh, hell

Unamused, the judge inscribed his own verse on the back of the document before committing it to the accumulated collection of official case records:

He danced all night
'till broad daylight,
And defended the whores in the morning.[43]

The State's criminal action against the four commenced on August 7 and continued through August 11. Counselor Berry's pathetic motions and objections were overruled at every turn. Cavner got 10 days in jail and a one hundred-dollar fine. George received a twenty-five-dollar fine. George believed the fine to be unjust and elected to appeal the judgement. Because he was to have been held in the County Jail until the fine was paid, Maggie was required to put up a five hundred-dollar surety bond for his release until the outcome of his appeal.

In comments made to the *Wellingtonian* concerning Maggie, Berry is quoted as saying, "that her only fault was—that she is intolerable curst [intolerably cursed], and shrewd and froward (sic): So beyond all reason, that were my state far worser than it is, I would not wed her for a mine (of) gold."[44]

8

George's appeal was never reconciled; for a week later with Cavner still serving time, and less than two months after Fred Kuhlman's death, Fred's benefactor met the same fate under remarkably similar circumstances, as reported in the Caldwell *Commercial.*

THE KILLING OF GEO. WOODS

About 8 o'clock on Thursday night of last week [August 18, 1881] the sharp report of a revolver started the general quiet of the city, and shortly after the news circulated that George Woods, the proprietor of the Red Light dance house and been shot and killed.

The account of the occurrence as given by the inmates of the house was about as follows: It appears that a young fellow named Charlie Davis, who came to Caldwell from Texas some time last fall, had been keeping a girl, an inmate of the house, who goes by the name of Lizzie Roberts. Davis had endeavored to induce the girl to leave the house and live with him. On Thursday night he went down there to get her to leave, and told her she must go with him. She refused, and Woods said she should not go unless she wanted to. Davis asked Woods what he had to do with it, at the same time calling him an opprobrious name. Woods replied, saying that he had a great deal to do with it, and ordered Davis to leave the house. Davis immediately pulled out his revolver and fired at Woods, the ball striking the latter between the breast bones and a few inches above the navel, going clear through his body and lodged in a partition a few feet behind where Woods was standing. Woods immediately grappled with Davis, seized the revolver and attempted to get it away from the latter. In the struggle the two got out of the front door and a few feet from the house, when Davis succeeded in getting away and ran up town, where he gave himself up to a policeman. Woods walked into the house and toward the back door, near which he laid or fell down, saying that he was killed. He was placed upon a cot in the room and Dr. Noble sent for, but the bullet had done its work and he only lived a short time after.

On Friday morning Judge Kelly summoned G.G. Godfrey, I.B. Gilmore, L. Thrailkill, S.H. Horner, H.C. Unsell and Wm. Morris as a coroner's jury and held an inquest upon the body. The testimony of the witnesses examined was taken down at length, but we were requested not to publish it. The jury rendered a verdict that George Woods came to his death from a pistol shot fired by the hands of Charlie Davis.

Davis, after giving himself up, finding that Woods was dead or about to die, concluded not to remain, and before provisions could be made for his safe keeping, gave his custodians the slip and got away. As there seems to be a sudden and great desire for the enforcement of all penal laws upon our statute books, we presume vigorous efforts will be made for his re-capture and punishment.

Of the two men, Woods and Davis, little need be said at this time.

Woods was well known in Wichita, Caldwell and Hunnewell. He had for several years kept a brothel in the first named place, removing to Caldwell last year, where he opened up the Red Light, and this spring set up another house in Hunnewell. Outside of his business he was generally well liked by those who knew him, and was said to be honorable and upright in all his business transactions. The occupation he followed was not such as to make him a very useful or ornamental member of society and his violent death is only regarded as a natural result.

Of Charlie Davis we know but little. We have seen him about town for nearly a year, and always as a quiet man. It is said by those who know him that he was not quarrelsome, seldom got under the influence of liquor, and never made a practice of carrying weapons. It is claimed by some that he was intoxicated on Thursday night, and by others that he was duly sober. Be that as it may be, he has perpetrated a crime which will practically make him a wanderer upon the face of the earth, and perhaps bring him to a violent death.[45]

Caldwell police records show that Davis had previously assaulted one Samuel Blacketer for which he was fined $7.50 exactly ten months to the day before killing Wood.

The *Post* offered much the same information as the Commercial:

THE SHOOTING SCRAPE

On last Thursday evening at about nine o'clock two shots were heard in rapid succession in the direction of the Red Light dance house, and soon a reporter from this paper was on the ground and found George Wood, proprietor of the house, lying on a cot in the dance hall, bleeding freely from a murderous looking hole in his breast, and writhing in fearful agony. Dr. Noble was doing all in his power to alleviate his sufferings, but it was of no avail. He had met his man and got his medicine.

To say the least, George has been the most successful dance-house man in the valley, so far as keeping an orderly house is concerned.

The circumstances of the shooting, as developed by the coroner's jury, are about as follows:

Charles Davis had been keeping Lizzie Roberts for some time, but about five weeks ago she left him and went to the dance house to live. Davis went to the house on this evening, and was insisting on Lizzie leaving the house and going up town to a room with him. This she refused to do. They were standing in the west room of the building, and George Wood was standing behind the bar. When the fuss commenced, he came around toward Davis, and told Davis he could not take the girl from the house unless she wanted to go. A few high words were passed, when Davis drew a Colt's improved forty-five revolver, and fired at about three feet range. The ball passed through Wood, and entered the partition back of the bar room. Wood grabbed hold of the revolver and hung onto it until he was dragged out of the house. They scuffled around in the yard a few moments, when another shot was fired but did not take effect on Wood. Wood was not armed. Nor was either man under the influence of liquor. Wood called his wife to him, and told her to "catch Charley Davis and prosecute him to the full extent of the law," and for her to keep all the property, do the best she could, and be a good girl. Charley Davis ran from the Red Light up the street toward town, and was captured and disarmed by Policeman Rowen, who turned him over to some one to guard until he went to the dance house to see what the row was about. The prisoner

escaped, and has not as yet been gathered in, that anybody knows of. Woods' friends buried him Friday after-
noon in the cemetery north of town. So ends the career of
the keeper of the Red Light.[46]

George had a history of carrying a concealed weapon. Had
he followed this habit on that evening, the outcome may have
been much different. But as it was, Governor St. John offered
a one thousand-dollar reward for Davis' capture and Maggie
offered five hundred-dollars.

Marshal Joe Dolan had paid $50 on his note but still owed
$155 when George was laid to rest. For reasons not totally
understood, George lay in a temporary grave for some time
after his death (as did Kuhlman.) The reason could be partially
due to some shady events surrounding the misappropriation
of a certain diamond stickpin (to be discovered later).

The question arises as to where that temporary location
was—the location given in the *Post* article is ambiguous
because the "cemetery north of town" could have been either
of the town's two cemeteries: the old cemetery is as far north
and *east* as the new one is north and *west*. In commentary
offered by researcher Richard Lane in his excellent 1984 edition of *Midnight and Noonday*, he suggests that George was
first interred at the Arnold cemetery, Caldwell's first cemetery
more commonly known in Caldwell as the "Boot Hill Cemetery."[47] It is curious why Maggie would have buried George at
that cemetery when the new cemetery had been in use more
than a year, since November of 1879.[48] It seems more likely
that interment would have been at the new cemetery.

Maggie had a Wichita marble firm fabricate a fine monument topped off with two columns made of Knoxville, Italian and Vermont marble. The piece had "taken the premium" at the Sedgwick County Fair and had cost Maggie $550, a full year's wages for the typical cowboy.[49] Lane suggests that the two columns and upper portion were lost when the grave was moved from "Boot Hill" to the new cemetery. The monument had been in place at the initial plot, wherever that was, at least before December of 1881. But whatever the case and for whatever reason, Maggie did not purchase the *final* resting place in the new cemetery until March of 1882, some seven or eight months after the murder.[50] She then buried George and Fred Kuhlman side by side in one of the most unique gravesites of that turbulent period to be found anywhere. There is a single monument, engraved with both names; both men having been saloon operators and pimps; both respectively being killed by a single bullet passing completely through the body; both dying in defense of Red Light prostitutes under their protection; both twenty-eight years old. The base of the monument and the remains of George Wood and Fred Kuhlman now reside at Block 03, Lot 0129, Spaces 2 and 3 in the (new) Caldwell City Cemetery.

George Wood/Fred Kuhlman Tombstone

The loss of the grand mogol of the demi monde, who was made an angel of at Caldwell the other night, does not seem to affect the dance house interests. "The dance still goes on."[51]

9

Shortly after Wood's murder, Maggie employed George Spear to manage the saloon portion of the Red Light. George was the older brother of David Spear, the suspected murderer of lawman Frank Hunt in the Red Light, mentioned earlier.

At the same time, a man alleged to be a bad Texas desperado moved into town. James Sherman, a.k.a. Jim Daniels, a.k.a. Jim Talbot was rumored to be the nephew of General William T. Sherman. Of much more consequence to the citizens of Caldwell, he was also reputed to be the cousin of Sylvester Powel, the man that Mike Meagher had killed in self-defense some four years earlier in the noted Wichita outhouse altercation.

Another story portrayed Talbot as the half brother of Caldwell's recently slain ex-marshal, George Flat. Earlier, Meagher, City Mayor at the time of Flatt's ambush, had been implicated as the suspected leader of the alleged assassination conspiracy. Whatever the case, Talbot, as he was known in Caldwell, was said to have loudly voiced his intention to kill Mike Meagher.

The *Post* reported that Talbot "generally gambles and carouses around saloons...He is wanted in several places for horse stealing and shooting men. Is a bad outlaw."[52] Shortly, he was joined by six confederates.

These men were desperadoes and were constantly giving the marshal trouble by their daring feats and the free use they made of their sixshooters. They visited the numerous places of amusement, accompanied by the prostitutes of the 'Red Light' dancing hall, and made disturbances by using loud, obscene language in the presence of ladies, or by their braggadocia, which they displayed while they were under the influence of whiskey. Talbot's men were frequent visitors of the 'Red Light', and several of the men were arrested and fined for creating a disturbance.[53]

Threats were made upon the lives of several of the townspeople. The gang's outrageous activities concerned the town so much that Mayor Cass Burrus, considering the situation incorrigible, deputized half a dozen or so men to bolster new Marshal John Wilson's effort to attenuate the gang's hold on the town. Several antagonistic incidents with guns drawn between gang members and the lawmen brought the showdown to a fever pitched impasse.

Then on Saturday morning, December 17, 1881, at about daybreak, as unbearable tension gripped the town, George Spear, manager of the Red Light Saloon since the death of George Wood, and avowed sympathizer of the Talbot faction, began firing his revolver in the street. Thus began the famous "Talbot Raid" one of the most momentous full-scale gun battles between bad men and townspeople in western history.

Talbot fiercely assumed command of his gang and according to Freeman, in *Midnight and Noonday*:

> …was standing on Main Street, when he began firing his revolver; his voice sounded in the air, "Hide out little ones!" A number of citizens armed themselves to assist the marshals. Each man armed with a gun or revolver were in hiding behind the stores, outhouses, and any place that would serve as a fortification or would shield them from the shots fired by the desperate Jim Talbot and his gang.[54]

At that time, when a new Winchester rifle cost $25 and a single action Colt revolver cost $12, the proprietors of two stores "handed out their stock of arms to the citizens as long as there was a gun left, without receipts and in many instances without knowing who was taking the guns. The two houses had about $800 worth of guns out."[55]

> The bold and fearless form of Jim Talbot was the center of the firing. He stood bravely to the front, with revolver in each hand, firing at the men he had premeditated to kill. Shots fired by the citizens were striking the buildings and tearing up the ground in all directions near the fearless leader who stood undaunted by shot or bullet, watching for the men who were to be his victims.[56]

After the battle had raged for some time, Talbot and Meagher focused their skirmish exclusively upon each other. Finally, after a violent gunfight among the buildings and alleys along Main Street, Meagher was felled by a fatal shot from Talbot's Winchester—barely half a block from the Red Light Saloon.

During the melee, Ex-mayor Hubble, anticipating their escape, determined to deprive the gang of the use of their horses. He secured his Winchester rifle, crossed the alley from the rear of his store and passed through A.C. "Lengthy" Jones' blacksmith shop, which fronted on Chisholm Street. From the front of Jones' shop, he commenced to shoot a block north up Chisholm at the gang's horses which were tied at the front of the Red Light, killing or disabling them.[57] It was during this time that George Spear was shot and killed while saddling one of these horses. Although contemporary Oliver Nelson, in his book, *The Cowman's Southwest*, says Spear was killed by a Winchester in the hands of a Deputy Marshal,[58] it appears more likely that a bullet from Hubble's rifle, intentional or not, did the deed.

All but two of Talbot's men made good their escape.

George Spear Tombstone

An inquest was held on the remains of George Speers, the jury finding that he came to his death by a gunshot wound in the breast from a gun in the hands of some person not known to the jury.[59]

The townspeople were enraged. A city resolution was passed to batten the door of, "that sink-hole of iniquity, the Red Light dance house."[60]

◆   ◆   ◆

The Talbot affair unnerved Maggie and feeling the city's hostility becoming more worrisome, she apparently considered a diversion as witnessed by the *Sumner County Press* in Wellington: "We are informed that it is her intention to set up an establishment in this city until affairs quiet down somewhat in Caldwell."[61] But the clamor did quickly settle down—the Red Light thrived in Caldwell and the turbulence continued unabated.

10

In May of the next year (1882), a grisly event came to light.

ROBBING THE DEAD

On complaint entered by Margaret Wood, Dave Sharp was arrested on Tuesday morning [May 16], charged with opening the grave in which George Wood's body was buried and taking from the corpse a diamond pin. An examination of the accused was had before J. D. Kelly, Esq., and the accused held to bail in the sum of $1,000 for his appearance at the next term of the District Court. He gave bail, Henry LeBreton [Owner of the Texas Saloon and Caldwell's most notorious professional gambler] becoming his bondsman.

The circumstances which led to the arrest of Sharp we understand to be about as follows. Last winter, shortly after the shooting matinee in which Mike Meagher was killed, a girl who goes by the name of Minnie, and who lived at the Red Light at the time of the shooting, informed Mag Woods that Blanche, another of the demimonde, who was living with George Spear at the time the latter was killed had told her, while they were in Kansas City that George Spear [manager of the Red Light Saloon whom Maggie had held in trust and who was shot while saddling a horse in front of the Red Light during the Talbot Raid] and Dave Sharp had opened George Wood's grave and taken the diamond pin from the body. The statement of the girl Minnie was given little attention until a few days ago, when Mag became impressed with the idea that the girl's story must be true, and on Monday night she had an interview with Blanche in which the latter gave all the details connected with the affair.

In summary, the article related Blanche's story:

...one night shortly after Wood was buried George Spear and Dave Sharp started out with a spade and some tools;...[Blanche] inquired as to where they were going.... Spear answered that they were going sky-larking. Not satisfied...she followed the men, who took a direct course for the cemetery;...finding the grave, they built a small fire by the side of it and began to dig...When they were fairly at work, Blanche went up to them and from that time was a close spectator of all that transpired. When the earth had been removed to the box which contained the casket, they broke the top off with a hatchet, then broke the lid and glass of the case, removed the diamond pin from the shirt front of the body, and then filled in the earth, never taking any trouble to fix the casket so that the dirt would not fall in upon the body...They also threw in the pieces of burning wood and coals of the fire they had kindled and returned to town.

After the arrest of Sharp, and at the request of Mag Woods,...[various officials] went to the cemetery to take up the body and examine it...The surface of the grave showed indications of having been disturbed, and as the removal of the earth proceeded, they found a piece of the lid of the coffin, then coals and burnt wood...and finally the broken box and the broken coffin. The coffin was taken out of the grave, the body removed from it and a strict examination made. There on the shirt front were the markes [sic] of the pin...[62]

The trial of Dave Sharp, charged with opening the grave of Geo. Wood and removing from the body a diamond pin, was concluded on Saturday last before P.H. Proctor, Justice of the Peace of Bluff Township and H.R. Harrington, J.P. of Caldwell Township. The testimony of Blanche Stevens was unsupported by any outside evidence whatever, and consequently Sharp was discharged.[63]

George Spear, successor to George Wood as keeper of the Red Light Saloon, is buried in the next plot north of his predecessor; the man whose grave he and David Sharp had ghoulishly violated in pursuit of the infamous diamond stick-pin. His stone reads "George Spear—Murdered."

In a bizarre twist of fate—three gunshot Red Light Saloon-keepers now lie in the Caldwell Cemetery—*three in a row.*

Three In A Row

11

On June 12, 1882, within a day or two of David Sharp's trial, Marshal George Brown, Caldwell's new lawman of barely two months, entered the Red Light and escorted Maggie to Judge J. D. Kelley's police court where she was fined for the seventh time in Caldwell for "running a house of ill repute."[64] It was to be Maggie's last arrest in Caldwell.

About a week later:

> On the morning of June 22nd, 1882, two Texans rode into the town of Caldwell. They put their horses in the livery stable and immediately went to a saloon where they filled themselves with the vile stuff known as whiskey. They soon made themselves conspicuous in the eyes of the citizens by the various feats which they displayed with their sixshooters.
>
> At last they seek the noted "Red Light," kept by the notorious Mag Woods, and there they indulge in drinking more whiskey and enjoying the society of the inmates of this vile den. They annoy the passing citizen by their profane and obscene language, and frighten the wives of the citizens who live in that immediate neighborhood, by the frequent firing of their sixshooters.[65]

Again, and for the last time, Marshal George Brown entered the Red Light; this time to stop the disturbance and to relieve the Texans of their six-shooters.

The Caldwell *Commercial* reported:

> Arriving at the Red Light, Brown and [Constable Willis] Metcalf proceeded up stairs, the former in the lead. On reaching the top of the stairs they found three men, one of whom had a pistol in his hand. Brown laid his hand on the man with the pistol and told him to give it up. The latter replied "let go of me," when Brown grasped hold of the fellow's arm and pressed it against the wall. Meantime, another man grasped Metcalf by the throat and backed him up into the corner, at the same time telling him to hold up his hands, the order being enforced by another who held a pistol at his head.
>
> Just then another man jumped out of a room across the stairway and to the right of where Brown and the man he was holding stood, and called out "Turn him loose." This seems to have attracted Brown's attention momentarily, but that moment was most fatal to him, for the man whom he held turned his wrist and fired, the ball from the weapon crashing through the Marshal's head, and he fell to the floor dead, without a struggle or a groan...
>
> On going to the Red Light, we found the body of George Brown at the head of the stairs, his face covered with a clot of blood and his brains spattered on the wall and floor of the building, while the gore dripped through the floor to the rooms below.[66]

The desperadoes rode hard south out of town, "on their way to the [Indian] Territory, the refuge for every fiend who perpetrates a crime upon the southern border of Kansas."[67]

The Wichita *Beacon* ran a graphic story similar to that above. The reporter, who seemingly had forgotten the attempt upon Mike Meagher's life in Wichita, was moved to end his write-up on the Brown murder with the observation:

> ...Caldwell is having a worse experience than ever Wichita had. We never had an officer killed, or even assaulted with deadly intent in all the wild days of the cattle trade here.[68]

12

A Caldwell temperance association with an attendance of about 100 had been in place by October 1880 although saloons were still legal. From its earliest days, Caldwell had officially condemned prostitution, but nevertheless condoned the brothels as a necessary evil, an essential inducement to insure continued cattle trade. Several unimpassioned attempts were made through the years to purge the harlotry from the town but their efforts were met by stiff resistance.

Three city ordinances which had been established were particularly troublesome to those vying to maintain an "open" city.

> Sec. 15. Any person or persons keeping, owning or conducting a house of prostitution or other place for the purpose of prostitution or lewdness within the corporate limits of the city, shall be fined in a sum not less than ten nor more than one hundred dollars.

> Sec. 16. Any and every inmate of a house of prostitution or other place of resort for prostitution and lewdness, shall be punished by a fine of not less than ten nor more than twenty dollars.

> Sec. 17. Any woman living in a hotel or tavern, or in apartments or rooms in this city, who shall entice or attempt to entice prostitution, or who shall follow the

calling of prostitution for gain, in the city, shall upon conviction, be fined and punished in like manner, and to the same extent as is now or may here-after be provided by ordinance, in the cases of inmates of houses of prostitution.[69]

An ominous letter was sent to the mayor voicing yet stiffer opposition. The letter was reproduced in the *Post*:

Dec. 26th 81
CALDWELL KS

CASS BURRUS

We think that you had better take a tumble to yourself if we let you go on you will imagen (sic) that you are a king our advice to you would be for you to resign from office We will give you 24 hours to eather (sic) remove those last ordinances No 14 No 15 No 16 or resign your office if within 24 hours you have not complied wit (sic) eather (sic) we will find some mode to remove you that wont be very satisfactory to your hide.

from the
K.K.K
Committee[70]

But the consensus of opinion in the city was steadily swinging to the position that the Red Light could no longer be tolerated. From its conception, it seemed hell-bent for oblivion. The murder of Marshal George Brown was the finale that brought the curtain down on the Red Light. Maggie had had enough of murder and mayhem. She put the Red Light up for sale.

Red Light for Sale

The property known as the "Red Light" is offered for sale. The house and lot will be sold separately or together. For particulars apply in the Savings Bank.[71]

Within a week, a consortium raised funds and purchased the Red Light:

Before the committee got half way around with the subscription paper last week, they had enough money ($400) to purchase the old Red Light building. It was purchased and deeded over to Wm. Corzine, who holds it for sale. When sold, the money will be divided pro rata among those contributing to the purchase fund. It has been closed up, the keeper of it, Mag Woods, going to Wichita, and the girls scattering out over the country, some taking private houses and others going to Wellington and Hunnewell. That old building has been the cause of more murders than any other house of the kind in the Southwest.[72]

◆   ◆   ◆

All of the bedlam, ferment, riot and carnage that caused such upheaval in Caldwell during the reign of the Red Light Saloon transpired in a span of just two and one half years.

◆   ◆   ◆

AFTERTHOUGHTS

A combine eventually bought the Red Light building to use for grain storage and moved it away from the original lot. By 1886 it had also served as a telephone exchange and an implement warehouse.

> Since the Red Light has been closed, we are at a loss to know what the tony young men, and older ones, for that matter of Wellington, who visit Caldwell for recreation, will do with themselves. We have always refrained from giving names or alluing to the matter when the aforesaid boys came to Caldwell and raised a little "hell" of their own; but in the future we shall give all such items of news for the benefit of those who slander our town and the cowboys. A cowboy has just as much right to get full and have a little fun as the toniest young man that Wellington affords, and if it lies in our power, we propose to lay the blame where it belongs.[73]

The company of the young ladies could still be had in Caldwell after Maggie's departure. Two bordellos continued to flourish. Dell Black's place at 107 Main Street was the next target of the city. But Poley Bright was by far the most nefarious baud in Caldwell. It is said "Poley Bright's place took the place of the old Red Light." The "entertaining" career of Poley

Bright, one of Maggie's original girls, outlasted any other in Caldwell. She was the third dove of that era to be arrested in Caldwell and was also the last when prostitution was finally purged in December of 1885. The record shows that she had more arrests by far than any other prostitute in Caldwell. Unaccountably, she was never fined as a madam.

By the latter part of 1885, Caldwell had finally become serious about putting an end to prostitution. The trail drives had dwindled, the town sought respectability and the last of the doves were flushed.

> The citizens of Caldwell propose to be as good as their word in driving out the hard cases from their town, and Mr. Sheriff Henderson's little brick boarding house received quite an acquisition from that city this afternoon to wit: Ellen Robinson, Laura Jones, Cola [Poley] Bright, and Fesse Phillips. They had a trial and were fined $100 each and six months in the county jail.[74]

◆   ◆   ◆

The *Sumner County Democrat* ran a puzzling piece in its September 29th issue of 1880: "Mr. and Mrs. Woods, the former proprietors of the 'Red Light' at Caldwell, are keeping hotel at Eureka Springs, Arkansas."[75] The time was less than two weeks before Frank Hunt was killed in the Red Light and it is known that the Woods were tending to their business in Caldwell in that time frame. It was found that deeds were not recorded at the Carroll County Courthouse in Eureka Springs before 1883 and no other record of the Woods can be found in Eureka Springs. The article remains an enigma.

◆   ◆   ◆

James Sherman, alias Jim Talbot, stood trial in Sumner County for the murder of Mike Meagher In April of 1895. He was acquitted. In case number 699, *The State of Kansas vs. James D. Sherman, alias James Talbot*, "Mag Wood" was among those listed as witnesses but did not appear.

◆   ◆   ◆

A document can be found in Fred Kuhlman's probate records wherein Maggie petitions the court to be allowed to sell the old Red Light building in Hunnewell. In the document, penned in May of 1884, she describes the property as being:

> ...unoccupied and has been for a number of months last past and that the same is deteriorating very much in value, that the same is becoming rickety; the windows and sash are being stolen and taken out, and that the same is liable to fall down during any hard storm which is liable to happen any day and that if said building remains where it is any considerable time it will become almost valueless except for fire wood; that to repair the same would be a greater expense that it could be sold for after the same should be repaired.[76]

◆   ◆   ◆

The railroad had reached Wellington ahead of Caldwell. In 1879, perhaps in anticipation of a boom in that town, George and Maggie purchased lots 17 and 18 in Block 58, the present site of the Knights of Columbus building in Wellington, Kansas. Their use of that property has been lost in time.

◆   ◆   ◆

Maggie commenced George's probate on August 22, 1881 but did not finalize it until July 7, of 1884. She also acted as "administratrix" for Fred Kuhlman, half owner and manager of the Hunnewell Red Light. The Notices of Final Settlement were first published in the *Post* on May 15, 1884. They were signed: "*Maggie Cavner*, formerly Margaret Ann Wood."

Notice of Final Settlement.

The State of Kansas, } ss.
Sumner County, }

In the probate court in and for said county.

In the matter of the estate of Fredrick Kuhlman, deceased.

Creditors and all other persons interested in the aforesaid estate, are hereby notified, that at the next regular term of the probate court in and for said county, to be begun and held at the court room in Wellington, county of Sumner, state of aforesaid, on the first Monday in the month of July, A. D. 1884, at 1 o'clock, p. m., I shall apply to said court for a full and final settlement of said estate.

MAGGIE CAYNER,
formerly Margaret Ann Wood, administratrix of Fredrick Kuhlman, deceased.
May 13th, A. D. 1884.   27t4

First publication, May 15, 1884.

Notice of Final Settlement.

The State of Kansas, } ss.
Sumner County, }

In the probate court in and for said county.

In the matter of the estate of George B. Wood, Deceased.

Creditors and all other persons interested in the aforesaid estate, are hereby notified, that at the next regular term of the probate court in and for said county, to be begun and held at the court room in Wellington, county of Sumner, state of aforesaid, on the first Monday in the month of July, A. D. 1884, at 2 o'clock p. m., I shall apply to said court for a full and final settlement of said estate.

MAGGIE CAYNER,
formerly Margaret Ann Wood, administratrix of George B. Wood, deceased.
May 13th, A. D. 1884.   27t4

First publication, May 15, 1884.

Notices of Final Settlement

On March 16, 1883, Maggie married Big Jim Cavner, the star of the Hunnewell altercation with Marshal Dolan. The ceremony was preformed in the Sumner County Court House at Wellington by none other than Judge Ike N. King, the same judge that had presided over the trial that had resulted from the Hunnewell fiasco a year and one-half earlier.

Perhaps the irony of the couple's return to his chambers rattled the judge—he listed Cavner's name where he should have inserted Maggie's. In effect, the resulting official Marriage License Record certifies that James Cavner had been legally joined in marriage to James Cavner.[77]

The 1885 Wichita Census lists Maggie A. Cavner, 28, Married; and on the next line James Cavner, 35, Married.[78] No occupation is listed for either. James came to Kansas from Fon du Lac, Wisconsin. The Cavners are shown to have owned the place where they lived at 141 Wichita Street which located them in the rough district about a block from the house where Maggie and George had started out a decade earlier.[79] Subsequent directories show them at the same address until 1888 at which time they owned their home at 216 Cleveland in Wichita. They have not been found after 1888.

◆   ◆   ◆

Caldwell's rowdy environment required extra tough men with exceptional courage to maintain law and order. The job was menacing and sometimes deadly. The formidable demands of the job were such that the lawmen didn't tend to stay on the job very long. In the six-year period from Caldwell's incorporation in 1879 through 1885, the year that saw the end of the major cattle drives to Caldwell, fifteen different marshals policed the streets of Caldwell.

Of those, the man with the greatest longevity, was Caldwell's most notorious lawman, Marshal Henry Newton Brown. In addition to having the longest tenure (Brown held the position nearly one and one half of those six years), it can be argued that he was the city's most effective lawman of that era and one of the most admired by the citizenry. Unbeknownst to all but a few of the townsfolk, Brown had been a close cohort of Billy the Kid and a veteran of the late "Lincoln County War" in New Mexico. On May 1, 1884, the people of Caldwell were shocked by the news that Marshal Brown, Assistant Marshal Ben Wheeler and a pair of accomplices, having attempted to rob a bank in Medicine Lodge, Kansas, had met violent deaths at the hands of irate citizens of that city.

Marshal Brown has been associated with Maggie in an instance that illustrates how events associated with noted historical personalities sometimes tend to loose a measure of objectivity with each retelling. An example is a scenario that relates a confrontation between Marshal Brown and Maggie:

> The Red Light's liquor license was revoked and Marshal Hendry [Henry] Brown ordered the place to be boarded up. Policemen were stationed there to bar anyone from entering or leaving. Mag screamed for justice, but to no avail. Marshal Brown informed her that she and her bawds had twenty-four hours in which to leave Caldwell voluntarily or be forcibly deported.
>
> The following afternoon the two-fifteen northbound local from Wichita stood at the depot, ready to pull out.

Several hundred spectators had gathered to watch the exodus of Mag and her whores. From where they stood, they could see the Red Light. It got to be two o'clock without any sign of movement in that direction. And then they saw the women coming down the slope carrying their suitcases, hurling a stream of obscenities and profanity at the gaping crowd. The conductor signaled the engineer several minutes later, and the train pulled out. Only then was the smoke rising from the Red Light noticed.

Mag wasn't there to enjoy the satisfaction of watching the place burn to the grown. But she had had the last laugh; before leaving, she had set the Red Light afire.[80]

A variation on the same theme:

[Marshal Henry Brown]...then went after Meg [Mag] Woods and her Red Light saloon and dance hall. Meg put up a spirited fight, but the decent townspeople backed the marshal and the city council declared the tavern a public nuisance and ordered it closed. As she left the place, Meg set it afire, and watched it burn as she and her "girls" pulled out of town on the train.[81]

And in another variation:

...[Marshals] Henry Brown and Ben Wheeler descended on the Red Light and hauled twenty men and women before Police Court Judge Reilley[82]

In reality, the Red Light was closed before Brown became Marshal—even before he became Assistant Marshal under Bat Carr and long before Wheeler was known to have come upon the Caldwell scene. Fire was not associated with the Red Light's demise and no record of Maggie's hostile departure can be found.

Another item, perhaps a well intended supposition, states that:

> ...George and notorious Mag Woods, husband and wife, and the vicious successors to Rowdy Joe and Kate Lowe, came down from Delano and built a two-story saloon, dance-hall, and bagnio on the corner of what is North Chisholm Street and East Avenue A.[83]

Actually, Delano in those days was a separate town across the Arkansas River west of Wichita. The Woods operated on Water and Wichita streets in the city of Wichita, not in Delano where Rowdy Joe's saloon was located. There is no known association between Rowdy Joe Lowe and the Woods. And it is now known that the Red Light was not located on Avenue A.

Another error appears in several accounts where veteran Ellsworth madam, Lizzie Palmer, has been confused with Maggie's alter ego, Lizzie Roberts and has been inserted into the Hunnewell Cavner/Dolan affair in place of Roberts.

Interestingly, Palmer had previously shown remarkable talent with what may be regarded as an unusually sensitive poem—considering her profession. The poem was to her estranged husband who had been suspected of arson in the torching of her "house" in Ellsworth.

Take Me Back Home Again

Take me back home again, take me back home,
Hopeless and helpless, in sorrow I roam;
Gone are the roses that gladdened my life,
I must toil on in the wearisome strife.
Once I was happy and friends were my lot,
Now I'm a wand'rer, despised and forgot!
Lonely and weary, in sorrow I roam,
Take me back home again, take me back home.

George, dear George, so gentle and mild,
Look once again on thy pitiful child!
Since we were parted I never have known
Love and affection so pure as thine own!
Days of my childhood, I dream of you now,
While in my sorrow and anguish I bow!
No one to love me 'neath yon starry dome,
Take me back home again, take me back home.

Oh, could I live but the days that are flown,
Dearest and sweetest that ever were known,
Fondly I weep in my desolate pain,
Longing to be with my George again!
Weary, so weary, my heart yearns for rest,
Poor wounded bird that is robbed of its nest!
Child of affliction! dear George, I come,
Take me back home again, take me back home.
Take me back home again, take me back home.

Theirs was a stormy relationship and again, in a month's time, he burned the new house she was living in—on the very day that she sent him the poem. He turned up murdered shortly thereafter.

◆　　　◆　　　◆

The complaint against Charlie Davis, Wood's murderer, is an interestingly comical study in redundancy:

> Now towit: on this 3rd day of February A.D. 1883 comes J. T. Herrick and files his complaint under oath charging that Charles Davis at and in Sumner County in the State of Kansas, on the 18th day of August A.D. 1883 in and upon one George Wood, unlawfully, felomausly [*sic*], wilfully [*sic*], deliberately, premediatatedly, [*sic*], and of his malice aforethought did make an assault, and that the said Charles Davis, a certain revolving pistol commonly called a revolver, there and then charged with gun powder and leaden bullets, then and there unlawfully, felomausly [*sic*], wilfully [*sic*], deliberately, premediatatedly, [*sic*], and of his malice aforethought did discharge and shoot off too against and upon the said George Wood and that the said Charles Davis with the leaden bullet aforesaid out of the revolving pistol aforesaid then and there by the fore of the gunpowder aforesaid by the said Charles Davis discharged and shot off as aforfesaid then and there unlawfully, felomausly [*sic*], wilfully [*sic*], deliberately, premediatatedly, [*sic*], and of his malice aforethought did strike, penetrate and wound the said George Wood in and upon and through the right side of the body of him the said George Wood, giving to said George Wood, then and there with the leaden bullet aforesaid so as aforesaid discharged and shot out of the revolving pistol aforesaid by the said Charles Davis in and upon and through the right side of the said body of the said George Wood one mortal wound of which said mortal wound the said George Wood, then and there instantly died: and

that the said Charles Davis the said George Wood with [?] and by means aforesaid, then and there unlawfully, felomausly [*sic*], wilfully [*sic*], deliberately, premediatatedly, [*sic*], and of his malice aforethought did kill; and [murder?] contrary to the form of the statue [*sic*] in such cases made and provided and against the Peace and dignity of the State of Kansas.[84]

Charlie Davis verdict

Charlie Davis had worked for rancher William Colcord not far from Corpus Christi, Texas, in the mid 1870's. In 1876, Colcord drove 1200 horses up the Chisholm Trail and eventually became one of three organizers of the Comanche Cattle Pool on the Cimarron River in the Cherokee Outlet.[85] Davis may have cowboyed at the Comanche Pool prior to Wood's murder.

◆   ◆   ◆

Noteworthy is the fact that the killers, Talbot, Stokley, and the Bean Brothers (the Beans were the killers of Marshal George Brown in the Red Light who claimed to have killed eighteen men between them, "not counting negroes") all sought refuge in the Indian Territory across the border two miles south of Caldwell. This was the standard practice of most all of the desperadoes that committed depravations in Caldwell and was bemoaned by the *Commercial*:

> If a man steals a horse and escapes into the Territory, he can be pursued, captured and returned to the state for trial and punishment. If he pulls out his little pop and shoots down a citizen, or an officer in the discharge of his duty, and once crosses the line between Kansas and the supposed home of the noble red man, the law rises up like a chinese wall and prevents any officer from following him. U. S. Troops also can be used to capture horse-thieves and remove settlers. But not the smallest atom of the U. S. Army may be devoted to the pursuit and arrest of an assassin, however heinous his crime. Unless a different system prevails, that same Territory will become such a stench and nuisance to the people of this border that no other interest or power will prevent them from changing its stance.[86]

Apprehension of such desperate characters within the Indian Territory was the business of a famed cadre of U. S. Marshals under the command of the noted "Hanging Judge" Isaac Parker headquartered in Fort Smith, Arkansas.

In a paradoxical turn of events, Fred Kuhlman's killer, Ed Stokley later became the protégé of famed Deputy U. S. Marshal Heck Thomas. In the summer of 1886, Sumner County Sheriff Thralls, after several fruitless pursuits, finally caught up with Stokley in Fort Smith and returned him to Wellington for trial. Stokley was found guilty of third degree manslaughter and served six months in the Sumner County lock-up at Wellington then returned to Fort Smith and a Deputy U. S. Marshal's commission. He returned to the Territory and continued his association with Marshal Thomas.

Deputy Marshal Ed Stokley was killed in the attempted apprehension of murderer, Will Towerly near Atoka, Indian Territory in 1887.[87]

"The Queen is dead—
        long live the Queen."

DEEDS

October 26, 1874   Volume 3, Page 314 (Sumner Co)

A.J. Dixon purchased from **Valentine Straub**

Lot #118 Chisholm Street (Original Town) Caldwell (and 27 others) for $300

September 21, 1875   Volume K, Page 525 (Sedgwick Co)

George Wood purchased from **Jas W. Parker**

Lot #44 Wichita Street (Munger Addition) Wichita for $15

March 11, 1879   Volume 14, Page 10

J.M. Wendels purchased from **A.J. Dixon**

Lot #118 (and 3 others) Chisholm Street (Original Town) Caldwell for $50

July 4, 1879   Volume 11, Page 70 (Sumner Co)

Henry R. Tumbaugh purchased from **J.H. Wendels**

Lot #118 (and 3 others) Chisholm Street (Original Town) Caldwell for $150

November 1, 1879   Volume 10, Page 328 (Sumner Co)

George Wood purchased from **J.S. Stacy**

Lots #17 & 18 in Block #58 Wellington for $35

February 9, 1880   Volume 12, Page 249 (Sumner Co)
J.W. Wendels purchased from **Henry R. Tumbaugh**
Lot #118 Chisholm Street (Original Town) Caldwell for $20

March 25, 1880   Volume 12, Page 535 (Sumner Co)
George Wood purchased from **John H. Wendels**
Lot #118 Chisholm Street (Original Town) Caldwell for $125

July 12, 1880   Volume 14, Page 436 (Sumner Co)
George Wood purchased from **Maggie Wood**
Lots #17 & 18 in Block #58 Wellington for $300

July 12, 1880   Volume 14, Page 48 (Sumner Co)
Maggie Wood purchased from **George Wood**
Lot #118 Chisholm Street (Original Town) Caldwell for $300

September 20, 1880   Volume 13, Page 583 (Sumner Co)
S.A. Bowerman purchased from **Sumner Co.**
Lot #118 Chisholm Street (Original Town) Caldwell for $0.18 back taxes

February 16, 1881   Volume 15, Page 63 (Sumner Co)
George Wood purchased from **Hunnewell Town Co.**
Lot #22, Block 33 Hunnewell for $120

May 11, 1881   Volume 17, Page228 (Sumner Co)

Fred Kuhlman purchased from **George Wood**

Lot #22, Block 33 Hunnewell for $450

July 19, 1881   Volume 17, Page 449 (Sumner Co)

George Wood purchased from **S.A. Bowerman**

Lot #118 Chisholm Street (Original Town) Caldwell for $25 (for clear title)

DEED NOT FOUND: Tax Deed for Lot #116 Chisholm Street (Original Town) Caldwell (Listed in the George B. Wood estate probate inventory.)

DEED NOT FOUND: Court ordered sale of Red Light/Lot #118 (and #116?) to William Corzine previous to June 6, 1882 .

December 6, 1882   Volume 29, Page 282 (Sumner Co)

B.F Munger purchased from **Willliam Corzine**

Lot #118 Chisholm Street (Original Town) Caldwell for $15

June 13, 1883   Volume 34, Page 225 (Sumner Co)

Charles W. Bennett purchased from **Maggie Cavner**

Lots #17 & 18 in Block #58 Wellington for $250

March 4, 1884   Volume 35, Page 264 (Sedgwick Co)

Maggie Wood Cavner purchased from **M.C. Hughson**

Lots #62, 64, 66 5th Avenue (JR Mead Addition) Wichita

Lease/Purchase $46 per month until $1500 has been paid

Septmber 18, 1886   Volume N/A, Page N/A (Sumner Co)

Mary Blackwood purchased from **Margaret Ann Cavner**

Lot #22, Block 33 Hunnewell for $450

BIBLIOGRAPHY

Barra, Allen, *Inventing Wyatt Earp*, Carrol & Graff, New York, 1998.

Bartholomew, Ed, *Wyatt Earp—The Untold Story.*

Butler, Anne M., *Daughters of Joy, Sisters of Misery*, University of Illinois Press, Chicago, 1985.

Colcord, Charles F. *The Autobiography of Charles Francis Colcord*, C C. Helmerich, Tulsa, Oklahoma, 1970.

Dobie, J. Frank, *The Longhorns*, Castle, Edison, NJ, 1941.

Drago, Harry Sinclair, *Notorious Ladies of the Frontier.* Dodd, Mead and Company, New York,1969.

———, *Wild, Wooly & Wicked*, Bremhall House, New York, 1960.

Dykstra, Robert R., *The Cattle Towns*, Alfred A. Knopf, New York, 1968.

Edwards, John P., Historical Atlas of Sumner County, Kansas, Philidelphia, 1883.

Emmert's   Wichita   City   Directory   and   Immigrants Guide—1878.

Erwin, Richard E., *The Truth About Wyatt Earp,* O.K. Press, Carpinteria, California, 1992.

Freeman, George. Midnight and Noonday—or the Incidental History of Southern Kansas and the Indian Territory—1871-1890, University of *Oklahoma* Press, Norman, 1984.

Lake, Stuart N., *Wyatt Earp—Frontier Marshal.* Boston, Houghton Miffin, 1931.

Martin, Cy, *Whiskey and Wild Women*, Hart Publishing, New York, 1974.

McLoughlin, Denis, *Wild and Woolly—Encyclopedia of the Old West*, Barnes & Noble, New York, 1975.

McNeal, T. A., *When Kansas Was Young*, Topeka, Capper Publications, 1940.

Miller, Nyle H., and Joseph W. Snell. *Great Gunfighters of the Kansas Cowtowns—1867-1886*, University of Nebraska Press, Lincoln, 1963.

———. *Why the West Was Wild*, Kansas Historical Society, Topeka, 1963.

Miner, Craig, *Wichita—The early years,* University of Nebraska Press, Lincoln, 1982

Nelson, Oliver, *The Cowman's Southwest*, H. A. Clark, Glendale, Califronia, 1953.

North, F.A., Comp, *Directory of the City of Wichita For 1885.*

————, *Directory of the City of Wichita For 1886.*

————, *Directory of the City of Wichita For 1887.*

————, *Directory of the City of Wichita For 1888.*

————, *Directory of the City of Wichita For 1889.*

O'Neal, Bill, *Encyclopedia of Western Gunfighters*, University of Oklahoma Press, Norman, 1979.

Pennington, Bill, Sedgwick County, Kansas Marriages—Books A Through D—May 7, 1870 To October 22, 1889, Wichita Public Library, 1986

Police Dockets, Caldwell City Records, Caldwell, Kansas Police Dockets, Wichita City Records, Wichita, Kansas

Ridings, Sam P., *The Chisholm Trail*, Grant County Historical Society, 1975.

Seagraves, Anne, *Soiled Doves—Prostitution in the Early West*, Wesanne Publications, Hayden, Idaho, 1994.

Williamson, Roger E., *Wichita Police Department—1871–2000*, Wichita Police Benefit Fund Association, Wichita, 2001.

Worcester, Don, *The Chisholm Trail*, Indian Head Books, New York, 1980.

Wrampe, Ann, *Wichita Township Soiled Doves*, Wichita Public Library History Series, 1987.

Yost, Nellie Snyder, *Medicine Lodge, Sage Books, Chicago, 1970.*

DOCUMENTS

Marriage Records, Book "B", Sumner County, Kansas

Probate Records, Fred Kuhlman Estate, Sumner County, Kansas

Probate Records, George B. Wood Estate, Sumner County, Kansas

United States Census, State of Kansas, County of Sedgwick, City of Wichita. 1875, 1880, 1885.

United States Census, State of Kansas, County of Sumner, City of Caldwell. 1880.

Revised Ordinances of the City of Caldwell, 1881

State of Kansas vs. Charles Davis, Sumner County Court Records.

State of Kansas vs. James D. Sherman, Sumner County Court Records.

State of Kansas vs. George Woods, Mag Woods, Lizzie Roberts and James Cavner, Sumner County Court Records.

NEWSPAPERS

Caldwell *Commercial*

Caldwell *Free Press*

Caldwell *Journal*

Caldwell *Post*

Caldwell *Standard*

Wellington *Sumner County Democrat*

Wellington *Sumner County Press*

Wichita *Beacon*

ARTICLES

Prostitution and Changing Morality in the Frontier Cattle Towns of Kansas.
By Carol Leonard and Isidor Walimann. Published in *KANSAS HISTORY—A JOURNAL OF THE CENTRAL PLAINS*, Volume 2, Number 1, Spring 1979.

Ed Stokley, Indian Territory Deputy U. S. Marshal.
By Edward Herring. Published in *OKLAHOMA STATE TROOPER*, Spring 2001.

ENDNOTES

CHAPTER 1

[1] Drago, *Wild, Woolly & Wicked*, p. 217
[2] Bartholomew, *Wyatt Earp—The Untold Story*, p. 96
[3] bid, p. 54
[4] Ibid, p. 54
[5] Interview with writer/researcher, Edward Herring
[6] Pennington, *Sedgwick County, Kansas Marriages*
[7] Drago, *Notorious Ladies of the Frontier*, p. 112

CHAPTER 2

[8] Colcord, *The Autobiography of Charles Francis Colcord*, pp 46, 47
[9] Seagraves, *Soiled Doves, Prostitution In the Early West*, p. 29
[10] Police Dockets, Wichita Records, Microfilm, Wichita Public Library
[11] *Emmert's Wichita City Directory and immigrants Guide*—1878, p. 96
[12] Bartholomew, *Wyatt Earp—The Untold Story*, p. 101

CHAPTER 3

[13] Drago, *Wild, Wooly & Wicked*, pp. 216, 217

[14] Caldwell *Post*, July 24, 1879

[15] Ibid, September 4, 1879

[16] Ibid, October, 30, 1879

[17] Ibid, June 3, 1880

[18] Police Dockets, Caldwell City Offices

[19] Deed—Volume 12, Page 535 (Sumner Co Courthouse) March 25, 1880 Lot #118 Chisholm Street—George Wood from John H. Wendels

[20] Caldwell *Post*, April 22, 1880

[21] Ibid, April 29, 1880

[22] Dykstra, *Cattle Towns*, p. 106

[23] Caldwell *Post*, May 20, 1880

[24] Ibid, June 17, 1880

[25] Ibid, May 13, 1880

[26] Ibid, May 20, 1880

[27] Ibid, May 20, 1880

CHAPTER 4

[28] Caldwell Messenger, July 24, 1939

[29] Freeman, *Midnight and Noonday*, 1984 edition, p. 203.

[30] Ibid, 1984 edition, p. 193.

[31] Probate Records, George B. Wood Estate

[32] Police Dockets, Caldwell City Offices

[33] Freeman, *Midnight and Noonday*, 1984 edition, pp. 196, 197.

[34] Caldwell *Post*, November 11, 1880
[35] Freeman, *Midnight and Noonday*, 1984 edition, p. 196.
[36] Colcord, *The Autobiography of Charles Francis Colcord*

CHAPTER 5

[37] Caldwell *Post*, October 14, 1882
[38] Caldwell *Commercial*, May 12, 1881

CHAPTER 6

[39] Sumner County Probate Court records, Fred Kuhlman estate
[40] Caldwell *Commercial*, July 7, 1881

CHAPTER 7

[41] Caldwell *Commercial*, August 11, 1881
[42] Ibid
[43] *Case #113, State of Kansas vs. Geo. B. Wood, et al,* Sumner County Court Records
[44] *Wellingtonion*, August 18, 1881

CHAPTER 8

[45] Caldwell *Commercial*, August 25, 1881
[46] Caldwell Post, August 25, 1881

[47] Freeman, *Midnight and Noonday*, 1984 edition, Lane footnote, p. 204
[48] Caldwell Post, November 6, 1879
[49] Sumner County *Press*, December 22, 1881
[50] Cemetery Records, Caldwell City Offices
[51] Sumner County *Press*, August 25, 1881

CHAPTER 9

[52] Caldwell *Post*, January, 4, 1883
[53] Freeman, *Midnight and Noonday*, 1984 edition, pp. 251, 252
[54] Ibid, p. 253
[55] Caldwell *Post*, December 22, 1881
[56] Freeman, *Midnight and Noonday*, p. 253
[57] Ridings, *The Chisholm Trail*, p. 477
[58] Nelson, *The Cowman's Southwest*, p. 33
[59] Caldwell *Post*, December 22, 1881
[60] Ibid, March 16, 1882
[61] Sumner County *Press*, December 22, 1881

CHAPTER 10

[62] Caldwell *Commercial*, May 18, 1882
[63] Ibid, June 15, 1882

CHAPTER 11

[64] Police Dockets, Caldwell City Offices
[65] Freeman, *Midnight and Noonday*, 1984 edition, pp. 207
[66] Caldwell *Post*, June 22, 1882
[67] Ibid, December 29, 1881
[68] Wichita *Beacon*, June 28, 1882

CHAPTER 12

[69] *Revised Ordinances of the City of Caldwell*, December,1881
[70] Caldwell *Post*, December 29, 1881
[71] Caldwell *Commercial*, June 22, 1882
[72] Caldwell *Post*, July 6, 1882

AFTERTHOUGHTS

[73] Ibid, July 6, 1882
[74] *Sumner County Press*, December 31, 1885
[75] Sumner County *Democrat*, September 29, 1880
[76] Sumner County Probate Court records, Fred Kuhlman estate
[77] *Sumner County Marriages*, Book "B", p. 224
[78] Federal Census, City of Wichita, 1885, p. 68
[79] Wichita City Directory, 1885, p. 39
[80] Rupp, *Notorious Ladies of the Frontier*, pp. 115, 116
[81] Yost, Medicine Lodge, p.92
[82] Drago, *Wild, Wooly & Wicked*, p. 265

[83] Drago, *Wild, Wooly & Wicked*, p. 250

[84] Court Records, *State of Kansas vs. Charles Davis.*

[85] Colcord, *The Autobiography of Charles Francis Colcord*, p 34

[86] Caldwell *Commercial*, June 29, 1882

[87] Herring, *Ed Stokley, Indian Territory Deputy U. S. Marshal, Oklahoma State Trooper*, Spring 2001, p. 55

0-595-29407-3

CPSIA information can be obtained at www.ICGtesting.com
Printed in the USA
LVOW10s1745120116

470290LV00001B/26/P